To Bob and Grace Burns

In fond memory of 1949-64

Lonnie

RELIGION
IN
RUSSIA TODAY

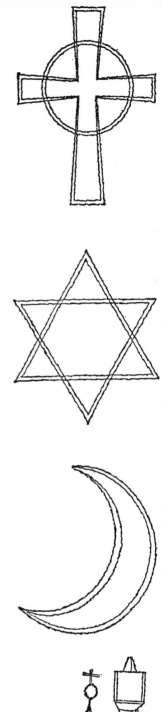

Religion in Russia Today

By ALONZO L. BAKER, Ph.D.

Professor Emeritus
University of the Pacific
Stockton, California

Professor, Political Science and History
Loma Linda University
Riverside, California, Campus

Southern Publishing Association

Nashville, Tennessee

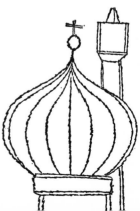

Copyright © 1967 by

Southern Publishing Association

Library of Congress Catalog Card Number: 67-28907

MANUFACTURED IN U.S.A.

TABLE OF CONTENTS

MARX VERSUS GOD

Chapter 1

The time: summer of 1965. The place: Yerevan Orthopedic Hospital, Soviet Armenia. I had traveled more than five thousand miles east to west across Siberia on the Trans-Siberian Railway, then down to the three Soviet republics lying between the Black and Caspian seas—Georgia, Armenia, and Azerbaijan. In Soviet Armenia I tumbled down a steep hill near Lake Sevan, six thousand feet high in the Caucasus Mountains. The fall broke the fibula and damaged some ligaments in my left ankle. Intourist phoned for an ambulance from Yerevan, Armenia's capital, fifty-five miles away. I was taken to the Yerevan Orthopedic Hospital and X-rayed. A cast was put on my lower leg, and I was placed in a private room at the hospital.

I was the first *Amerikanski* ever to be admitted to that hospital. As such I was the source of much curiosity on the part of the ambulatory patients and hospital employees. Because it was August, the weather was warm and the hall door to my room was open most of the time for cross-ventilation. Through this open door came a constant stream of onlookers to see an *Amerikanski*, many of them never

9

having seen that particular species of the human race before. Inasmuch as none of them spoke English and my Armenian vocabulary was confined to six simple words, dialogue and communication were a bit limited. But some of my viewers were on crutches or in wheelchairs, and this forged a bond between us as I showed them my cast. Sympathy, like music, is a universal language, spoken from the heart, and needs no tongue for communication.

One afternoon five college students were ushered into my room—three young men, two girls. These youths were students in a Yerevan college. All spoke English—not Harvard or Oxford English, but adequate English. Soon we were engaged in a lively two-hour conversation.

As is invariably the rule among the 235,000,000 persons who make up the Soviet Union, these young people were very friendly, and, of course, intensely curious about America and Americans. Every Russian—whether he lives in Nahodka or Khabarovsk in far eastern Siberia, or in the western Baltic republics of Estonia, Latvia, and Lithuania, or in the south along the Black Sea coast, or in central Asia's fabled cities of Tashkent and Samarkand—is ready instantly to ask a hundred questions of any American.

The five college students vied with each other in plying me with queries. Their prefatory remark was, "We heard there was an *Amerikanski* college professor in the Orthopedic Hospital; we wanted very much to see him, for we have never before seen an American college professor."

After that their interrogations came at me in waves.

"What do you teach? How much are you paid?"

"Where in the United States is your college?"

"Is your college coeducational?"

"Does your college charge fees, or is it free like all our colleges, universities, and institutes in the Soviet Union?"

"What kind of apartment are you furnished by your college? What rent do you pay?"

"How much did you pay for that suit of clothes hanging there? How much for your shoes?"

After the initial barrage of questions had subsided, I told the youths my college is not owned and operated by either the state or national government but is a private school and "church related." I had to explain that latter phrase, for of course there are no church-related colleges in the U.S.S.R. I told them we have various types of higher educational institutions in the United States—private and public, some financed and operated by the state government, some by private secular groups, some by Christian denominations, some by Jewish organizations.

This revelation seemed to mystify my auditors, for in the Soviet Union they live under a system where the all-powerful national government owns, operates, and controls everything. Nonuniformity and variety are concepts largely alien to the thinking of a Soviet citizen.

But what bowled the five students over was this:

"In the type of college where I teach, belief in God and in the values of religious experience is interwoven and integumented with the sciences, the arts, the humanities—in fact, with all educational disciplines."

"Do you mean," one asked in astonishment, "that you, a professor with a doctor's degree, really believe in God?"

"Oh, yes," I said; "very much so. I happen to hold the view that belief in God is the foundation, the substratum, of all worthwhile education."

"Do all college professors in America agree with you?"

"By no means," I replied. "Some do; some do not. However, in the church-related college where I teach all faculty members hold convictions akin to mine. But in our great state universities and in many private colleges it is immaterial whether a member of the faculty is a believer or not. He may be a faithful adherent of the church, or he may be a freethinker, even an atheist."

Then one of my five young friends ranged alongside my bed in the Yerevan Orthopedic Hospital made this significant statement:

"Well, in the Soviet Union no teacher, no college professor, would ever be allowed to stand before a class of students if he were so unscientific and reactionary as to believe religion is anything but a superstition, a tool of exploitation of the working class used by the privileged hierarchy of the church, which is always allied with the capitalist power structure and the ruling class."

In that categorical statement of Soviet dogma and policy the young Russian was altogether correct. The Soviet Union has sixty or seventy million students in the educative process, yet not one student ever sits under a teacher who is a believer. None but unbelievers ever stand behind a professorial lectern. There are no exceptions.

Furthermore, since the materialist philosophy and antireligious viewpoints are integrated into the curriculum of every school in Russia from the kindergarten through graduate study, all teachers must attack religion daily in the classroom. This is required.

Russia's Communist Party, consisting currently of eleven or twelve million members, allows no one to join unless he is a professed and an aggressive atheist. Affiliation with the Party is eagerly sought, for Party members command the best jobs and the best salaries, they are assigned the best apartments, and they are eligible for promotion to the higher echelons of political and governmental service. Party membership carries with it great social prestige and acceptance. But all Party members must be avowed atheists.

Atheism is likewise a requisite for membership in the Komsomol, the Young Communist League. This major Communist organization has presently a membership of some twenty-five million, all Communist youth ages seventeen to twenty-five. The Komsomol is often called "The Junior Communist Party," for from its membership are recruited most of the new members of the senior Communist Party, the CPSU—Communist Party of the Soviet Union. The CPSU is the nexus of all power in the Soviet Union. The CPSU is controlled by a Central Executive Committee of about 170 members, the core of which is the eleven-member Politburo, or Party Presidium. This Politburo is the real focus of all power for all Russia. From the Politburo flows all legislative, executive, administrative, economic, social, and political authority for the U.S.S.R.

The CPSU is highly selective in its membership. Overnight it could have a membership list of a hundred million or more if it were not kept small by deliberate design and policy. Lenin, the founder of the Soviet Union, declared that the CPSU should never number more than 3 percent of the total population of the country. Currently the percentage runs about 5 percent, owing to the necessity of enlarging the membership during the war against Hitler to get more Party workers for the war effort. Lenin said only the most ardent, the most dedicated, Communist should be taken into the Party. Party membership undergoes constant revision to weed out drones, lacklusters, dissidents.

The CPSU runs the Soviet Union, lock, stock, and barrel. One of its basic goals is the complete elimination of religion. Under both Lenin and Stalin bitter war was waged against all forms of religion—Orthodoxy, Roman Catholicism, Islamism, Buddhism, Judaism, and all variants thereof. However, after Hitler renounced his alliance with Stalin and attacked Russia in June, 1941, the Russian premier, Joseph Stalin, found it expedient, yes, even necessitous, to relent a bit in his campaign against religion, for he direly needed the support of all religionists to hurl back the immense weight of Hitler's minions. The "Great Patriotic War," as the Russians call the war against Hitler, marked a definite letup in the relentless attack against the Orthodox Church, the Latin Church, Judaism, Islamism, the Evangelicals, the Baptists, the Lutherans, the Seventh-day Adventists, and all other religionists.

This lessening of overt antagonism must not be interpreted as an alteration in the basic attitude of the Soviets toward religion. The new policy beginning with 1943 is one of temporary toleration only, a tactical expedient for a limited time. Eventually religion must go.

The Soviets believe time is on their side in the war against God. They affirm that religion survives in Russia mainly among two groups: (1) the elderly who were adherents of religion before the Revolution of 1917. Theirs is a generation soon to pass from the scene. (2) The peasants. But the number of peasants is fast decreasing; they are flocking into the cities to work in industry as agriculture becomes increasingly mechanized. In the cities they become proletarianized and secularized. When they leave the countryside, they leave God behind, say the Soviet leaders.

But more important in the war against religion, according to the Party leaders, all Soviet children begin attending state schools at age seven, where all students are given a thorough grounding in the fundamentals of materialism as a life view. In the course of their education they are shown how unscientific and antiscientific religion is, how it has always been used to exploit the working class, how the clergy have been the lackeys of the capitalists, and the church a coexploiter of both workers and peasants.

Thus, say the Soviets, because of universal education the younger generations have no faith in religion or in the church; therefore, with the older generation dead and gone and the newer generation wholly wed to Marxist materialism, religion will inevitably cease to be. It will die a natural death by the process of attrition.

But religion has a vitality that preserves it from destruction no matter how potent the forces marshaled against it. In all historical periods religion has evidenced a longevity which enables it to survive all who sentence it to death.

Why does Russia, and indeed all Communist peoples, put the extermination of religion high on their agendas?

Karl Marx denounced religion as the opiate of the people. This dogma has been sedulously espoused by Marxists for more than a long century. Marx (1818-1883), the founder of "Scientific Socialism," or communism, averred capitalism the taproot of all the world's ills. He said capitalists use religion to anesthetize the workers and toilers of the world so that they will not sense the nature and extent of their exploitation. The anesthetizing factor, say all Marxists, is the "pie in the sky by and by" doctrine. According to the Marxists, the clergy tell the economically deprived multitudes, "Poverty, injustice, illiteracy, and disease are all a part of God's plan for humanity in the present evil world; but if you are faithful in your religious vows and obligations, when you die, you will be transported to heaven, where you will walk streets paved with gold; for all eternity you will have everything your heart desires, with none of the deprivations afflicting you now."

Marxists often use the Holy Scriptures of Christianity to prove their point. They cite the New Testament writer

James to substantiate the view that religion is an opiate for the working class. Here from the J. B. Phillips Translation are the first nine verses of chapter 5 of the Book of James:

"And now, you plutocrats, is the time for you to weep and moan because of the miseries in store for you! Your richest goods are ruined; your hoard of clothes is moth-eaten; your gold and silver are tarnished. Yes, their very tarnish will be the evidence of your wicked hoarding and you will shrink from them as if they were red-hot. You have made a fine pile in these last days, haven't you? But look, here is the pay of the reaper you hired and whom you cheated, and it is shouting out against you! And the cries of the other laborers you swindled are heard by the Lord of Hosts himself. Yes, you have had a magnificent time on this earth, and have indulged yourselves to the full."

Then James goes on to exhort those who have been swindled by the plutocrats: "But be patient, my brothers, as you wait for the Lord to come. . . . Don't make complaints against one another in the meantime." [1]

The Marxists chortle over this Biblical passage, for, say they, James was giving the oppressed classes of his time a hypodermic injection of an opiate which would dull the pain of their oppression by the rich, swindling plutocrats. The oppressed must not complain but rather wait until heaven for their reward, a classic example, the Marxists allege, of the "pie in the sky by and by" doctrine of Christianity. Marx said the workers of the world are entitled to their pie now, not later in an uncertain and nebulous heaven.

Karl Marx was a voluminous writer. On page after page, in chapter after chapter, he developed the theme that the church has uniformly been on the side of the exploiters; very seldom, if ever, on the side of the exploited. His *magnus opus, Capitalism,* was written in London, where he lived from 1850 until his death in 1883. He cited the in-disputable fact that the Anglican Church, the state church of England, itself a wealthy institution, was inextricably bound up with wealth and privilege and with the aristocracy of Britain. He cited the feudalism of Europe, wherein the Roman Catholic Church was often the handmaiden of the landed and wealthy class, itself having vast estates.

The theories of Marx remained only theories until thirty-three years after his death, when Lenin and Trotsky took over czarist Russia. The Russians were the first people ever to put Marxism into operation. Lenin, the leader of the Soviet Revolution, accepted Marx and his theories 100 per-cent. He firmly believed religion to be the opiate of the people, that in order to destroy capitalism and capitalists in Russia religion must be destroyed root and branch. He knew, however, that the church was so deeply entrenched that it could not be done away with by simply decreeing it outlawed. Lenin, a shrewd and able leader, decided to put the church to death by degrees. The second month after the Soviets seized power Lenin and his fellow commissars decreed the separation of the church from the state. We give excerpts from the decree promulgated January 23, 1918:

"The Church is separated from the State. . . .

"The School is separated from the Church. Instruction in any religious creed or belief shall be prohibited in all State, public, and also private educational establishments in which general instruction is given. . . .

"All Church and religious associations are subject to the ordinary legislation concerning private associations and unions. They shall not enjoy special privileges, nor receive any subsidies from the State or from local autonomous or self-governing institutions. . . .

2

"No church or religious associations have the right to own property. They do not possess the rights of juridical persons.

"The property of all church and religious associations existing in Russia is pronounced the property of the People."

Shortly thereafter the Soviet commissars issued directives implementing the January decree. Among other stipulations were these:

All churches and religious associations are to hand in a complete inventory of all their properties, moneys, and assets within a fortnight.

All properties of religious groups, properties yielding a profit, such as landed estates, industries, factories, hotels, hospitals, etc., are to be confiscated by the state, such confiscation to be consummated within sixty days.

All books, records, and registers kept by religious groups and having to do with births, marriages, and deaths are to be turned over to the state.

In a short time many of the churches, synagogues, mosques, and chapels taken over by the state were closed; others were converted into recreation centers and social clubs, meeting places for Communist Party rallies, or warehouses and storage facilities.

Thus early in the Soviet regime the state sought to cripple religion with the avowed intent of doing away with it entirely in due time. The commissars pledged themselves to the total elimination of religion by the substitution of Karl Marx for God. They were determined to supplant the cross with the hammer and sickle.

---

[1] From The New Testament in Modern English. Copyright, J. B. Phillips, 1958. Used by permission of The Macmillan Company.

RELIGION COMES TO RUSSIA

Chapter 2

Tuesday, Vladimir was a hard-nosed pagan; Wednesday, Vladimir was a professing Christian.

"Oh," you say, "Vladimir had gone to a Billy Graham revival Tuesday night and was converted."

No, that is not at all the way it happened; for, you see, this occurred quite some time before Billy Graham was born —in fact, in the year A.D. 988.

Vladimir (rhymes with redeemer) ruled Russia 977 to 1015. It was he who brought Russia officially into the fold of Greek Orthodox Christianity. Vladimir, known in Russian church history as Saint Vladimir, was by no means the first professing Christian in the land of the Russ. Long before Vladimir was born, Christian missionaries, such as Cyril and Methodius, had made converts in Russia. Some Russians had accepted Latin Christianity, headed by the pope in Rome; others Greek, or Byzantine Christianity, headed by the patriarch in Constantinople.

Neither was Vladimir the first Russian ruler to turn his back on paganism: Princess Olga, ruler of Russia 945 to 962, had been baptized into Greek Orthodoxy in the year

955. In vain she sought to make a Christian out of her son and successor, Sviatoslav; he refused, declaring he was afraid he would be laughed at!

But a third of a century later when Vladimir became a Christian, he accepted religion not for himself alone, for, by decree, he took all Russians into the church with him whether they liked it or not, whether or not they understood the significance of what they were doing—into the church en masse they came. He ordered them down to the Dnieper River for baptism, and into the river they went by the thousands. When they came out of the water, they were Christians—just like that. This is what the advertising geniuses of Madison Avenue would call "instant Christianity"!

One of the amazing aspects of Vladimir's "conversion" was the fact that almost up to the day he became a Christian he was a crusading pagan and militantly anti-Christian. All the Russian peoples had a pagan background. When Rurik the Scandinavian organized the many tribes along the River Road into a nation in the year A.D. 862, they were all religious primitives and animists. They had many gods, all of them the gods of nature—gods of the sun, the thunder, the storm, the snow, the cattle, etc. They knew nothing else. By the next century, however, when Vladimir was ruler, many of Russia's neighbors had gone Christian, such as the Poles and the Liths to the west; or Islamic, such as the Bulgars along the Danube; or Jewish, such as the Khazars to the south. It became the "in" thing, the voguish thing, to do, to accept some formal religion in Vladimir's time.

The Varangians, or Scandinavians, to the north were likewise pagan in those days. These Northmen, one of whom was Rurik, who welded Russia's tribes into a nation, regularly traversed the River Road through Russia. The

River Road for Rurik began where the Western Dvina River emptied into the Baltic. Rurik and his countrymen went up the Dvina to its headwaters, then, portaging a few miles, they came to the headwaters of Russia's mighty Dnieper. They sailed down through Kiev and on to the Black Sea, thence to Constantinople. At that time Constantinople was the world's major trading center. It was the world's richest city, richest not only in material wealth, but richest in culture also. By all criteria Constantinople was City No. 1 in the world of the tenth century. The Scandinavians were not interested in culture, but they were interested in trade; hence their regular travel north and south along the River Road through Russia. From the Russians they bought furs, wax, and honey, carrying these on to Constantinople. On the return trip northward they sold the Russians articles of world commerce they had obtained in the big city on the Bosporus.

Vladimir, however, wanted to deal with Constantinople direct, not through the middlemen from Scandinavia. His people were doing some business already with the Byzantine merchants, but Vladimir wanted this business to expand. And this is one reason, perhaps the major reason, why Vladimir accepted the religion of Constantinople: to expand business for his people in the principal marketplace of the world. In other words, crass as it may sound, Vladimir's basic motivation was economic, not a seeking after better gods or more spirituality for his people.

And, too, there was another angle: Emperor Constantine in Constantinople promised Vladimir his beautiful sister as a wife if he accepted Greek Orthodoxy. Vladimir knew such a matrimonial alliance with the family of the monarch of mighty Byzantium would be no handicap to the would-be Russian merchant tycoons.

But Vladimir was a canny chap. Before he announced for Greek Orthodoxy, he went through all the motions of evaluation and impartial assessment. He invited the spokesmen for Roman Catholicism, Orthodoxy, Islamism, and Judaism to send representatives with arguments for the acceptance of their respective faiths.

Vladimir decided against Judaism because it forbade the eating of pork and made circumcision of all males compulsory. "We like our pork too much to give it up; and besides, circumcision is too messy and too painful. No, we cannot accept Judaism," he said to the Khazar envoys.

Vladimir decided against Islamism because the Koran forbade wine drinking: "We Russians must have our wine, you know."

Vladimir decided against Roman Catholicism on the basis that the pope claimed supremacy over secular rulers; Vladimir, as might be expected, wanted no one outranking him.

Before he announced publicly for Orthodoxy, Vladimir sent envoys to Constantinople to observe Greek Christianity firsthand. They went to the Cathedral of Saint Sophia and soon found themselves entranced with the beauty of the liturgy and with the antiphonal *a cappella* singing. To be sure, the city of Constantinople itself overwhelmed the emotions of these commissioners from the rough frontiers of the steppe lands of Russia. Constantinople, astride the Golden Horn, a great populous metropolis of maturity, beauty, luxury, culture, and sophistication, would have won them over even if there had been no Saint Sophia with its magnificent heavenly music. It is said that "music has charms to soothe a savage breast." It surely charmed the savage pagans from the hinterlands of the Russ.

Reporting to Vladimir upon their return, they were

unanimous in recommending he accept Orthodoxy, the religion of Saint Sophia and Constantinople.

His survey committee's report buttressed the private decision Vladimir had already made. Straightway he announced Russia would be Christian after the model of Byzantium. The patriarch sent him congratulations from Constantinople, assuring him that his choice would have made his grandmother, Olga, most happy, if she could only know of the Christianization of her grandson.

In the heyday of his paganism Vladimir had erected in front of his palace statues of many of the pagan gods: Perun, the god of thunder; Svarog, the father of gods; Veles, the patron of cattle; Stribog, the wind god; Dazhd-Bog, the sun-god; and many others. The very day he accepted Christianity Vladimir ordered that these statues be destroyed. No procrastinator was he!

As of now, Russia has existed as a nation for more than eleven hundred years, yet it is no extravagance to state that no other single event has influenced Russian civilization and culture more than Vladimir's avid espousal of Greek Orthodoxy in the year 988. To be sure, it now appears that religion as a dominant factor in Russian life suddenly was aborted the night of November 6-7, 1917, when the Soviets took over in the name of Karl Marx. But not a few contemporary historians hold the conviction that despite the avowed determination of the Kremlin men to extirpate all religion, belief in the Eternal is not destined to disappear from Russia as have the dinosaurs and troglodytes of former ages. They believe faith in God will someday undergo a renaissance in the U.S.S.R. and will again become a vital force in Russia's way of life, not in any union with the state, but autonomous and standing on its own feet. Those holding this view refuse to believe God is dead in that land, which covers one sixth of the surface of our globe and is the habitation of a quarter billion of its peoples.

What beneficent things did Orthodoxy do for Russia?

Orthodoxy gave Russia an alphabet and a written language.

Orthodoxy gave Russia new and higher concepts of morality and justice.

Orthodoxy gave Russia the Sacred Scriptures, the Old and New Testaments.

Orthodoxy gave Russia a religious art, as exemplified in its fabulous icons, and a distinctive church architecture.

Orthodoxy gave Russia its glorious religious music.

Orthodoxy gave Russia a literate clergy, who fostered education, libraries, and the production of literature.

Orthodoxy was the umbilical cord connecting backward Russia with the advanced culture of Byzantium.

In the year 1054 came the irreparable break between the Eastern and Western branches of Christianity, between Roman Catholicism and Greek Orthodoxy. In the long view the Eastern Church suffered greatly from this schism, for the bitter rivalry between East and West virtually isolated Russia from Western Europe for centuries. This, combined with two and a half centuries of domination by the Mongol Tartars (1223-1480) transformed Russia into a hermit nation, introvert and recessive. At the same time Europe was undergoing the Renaissance and the Protestant Reformation. Russia knew nothing of the rebirth of learning and of the great progress made by Europe in science, politics, and economics. While it is true that both Peter the Great and Catherine the Great tried to break Russia's isolationism by opening windows on Europe, yet they came along too late to undo most of the damage done by centuries of aloofness and separation from the main currents of life in Europe. Russia stagnated at the very time Europe was on the *qui vive*.

In the fifteenth century (1453) the Turks captured Constantinople, destroying the Byzantine Empire. The fierce fighting forces of Islam for a time threatened all Europe. The Orthodox Church had no choice but to move its patriarchal headquarters far to the northeast into Russia, eventually headquartering in Moscow. Soon the city on the Oka was recognized as the center of world Orthodoxy.

In time Moscow became known as "the Third Rome." This phrase was coined by the Monk Philotheus of Pskov. Philotheus said "the First Rome" on the Tiber was for centuries the world's repository of truth. But "the First Rome," he said, "fell into grievous error in the schism of 1054." Then "the Second Rome" came into being in Constantinople. The patriarchate of Greek Orthodoxy then became the center of truth for the world. So long as it preserved God's holy truth in pure form, "the Second Rome" prospered. But it, too, succumbed to error and paid for its sin by falling prey to the infidel Turk. Thereafter the torch of truth was carried to Moscow, which became "the Third Rome." "There will be no 'Fourth Rome,' " Philotheus said, "for light and truth have found their eternal home in Moscow."

Little did the Monk Philotheus foresee the vicissitudes and reverses the church would suffer under the Romanovs. Little did he dream of the lethal bludgeonings and near-death existence of the church under the Soviets.

When the Orthodox Church came to Russia under the sponsorship of Vladimir, it was made the official state church. Vladimir was most careful never to allow the church the upper hand; that was his alone. He, the symbol of state power, exercised supremacy at all times over the hierarchy and every phase of ecclesiastical affairs. The church, however, was honored by Vladimir. It received generous state subsidies; this put God in Caesar's debt. Dependency always means subserviency.

Russia's rulers held the power of appointment of the patriarch, the metropolitans, the archbishops and the bishops of the church; that is to say, the state held the power of veto over all nominations of high officials in the church. On the other hand, the czars were crowned by the patriarch under church auspices and authority akin to the role of the Anglican Church in the coronation of Britain's ruler today.

All this does not mean that relations between the church and state in Russia were always harmonious, for it will be remembered that Peter the Great abolished the patriarchate and sacked the patriarch; he was, in turn, excommunicated by the church. The church even labeled Peter "the antichrist."

In place of a patriarch Peter organized a Holy Synod to conduct all church affairs. The Synod was run by a secular official appointed by Peter, the procurator-general. For nearly two hundred years (1721-1917) the church was run by a procurator-general, an official named, controlled, and directed by the state.

Do I hear you query, What was the cause of the big break between the church and Peter the Great?

It began before Peter was born. About the middle of the seventeenth century the church was rent with internal criticism and dissension. At that time the monastic orders owned vast lands and had amassed great wealth. Some of the younger clergy coming on felt that the church had lost sight of its mission in the world and was interested only in wealth and prestige. They alleged spirituality had declined as the sums of wealth went higher and higher. They declared the monastic orders had become far more interested in lands and money than in the souls of men.

Taking cognizance of this ferment and criticism in the church, state authorities in 1649 established a new department which was to have control of all the secular activities of the church. This department soon blocked any further expansion of church lands. Some of the special privileges of the clergy and monastic orders were curtailed.

In the year 1652 the presiding patriarch died, and a young forty-two-year-old patriarch was appointed—the Patriarch Nikon (1652-1666). Nikon was very able, very personable, a man of impeccable piety and devotion to the church. Among other firm convictions Nikon believed the church was much in the need of reform, many reforms. Being a linguistic scholar of considerable reputation, Nikon was irked by the many mistranslations and errors in the Slavonic Bible and in the Service Books of the church. When Vladimir was converted in the tenth century, he was most anxious to have the Bible and the liturgical books then in use in Constantinople translated for use in Russia; he commanded that this should be done immediately, if not sooner! Haste makes waste, and haste causes translators to make endless errors.

Every time Nikon opened the Bible or the liturgical books, his eyes fell on error after error. Now that he was patriarch, he decided the errors should be eliminated.

When translating the word *Jesus* in the Slavonic, the hurried translators spelled it "Isus." The correct spelling was "Iisus." Half a millennium had come and gone by the time Nikon assumed the patriarchate, but he declared five hundred years do not minimize a major mistake in translation. So he ordered new translations with the spelling "Iisus."

The great majority of church members in Russia were at that time illiterate and totally oblivious to spelling, be it correct or incorrect. But some of the clergy declared "Isus" was the Russian word for Jesus, and any change would be blasphemous and sacrilegious. Multitudes of the people and many of the clergy rose in revolt against this Nikon reform in spelling.

Another reform demanded by the patriarch was a change in the number of fingers used by priests in crossing themselves and in giving the blessing. In Constantinople the rule had been three fingers, signifying the Trinity—God the Father, God the Son, and God the Holy Spirit. But the Russian clergy had adopted the two-finger blessing, saying the two fingers represented the dual nature of Christ as He hung on the cross—human and divine.

Then there was a heated debate whether religious processions should move with the sun or against the sun, whether "hallelujah" should be repeated two times or three times in the liturgy, whether the Russian church should continue to use icons influenced by the Latin church or go back to the pure Greek form.

The leader in the bitter opposition to Nikon was an archpriest, Father Avvakum (1620-1682).

To us living in the twentieth century the huge eruption and schism in the Russian church when Nikon ordered these reforms appears nothing more than a tempest in a teapot, a disagreement over nonessentials. In seventeenth-century Russia, however, these issues assumed a life-or-death importance; a man's salvation or his eternal damnation depended on his stand on these matters.

Those who wanted no change, no reforms, were called *Raskolniki,* or "Old Believers." Believe it or not, hundreds of thousands, perhaps a million, Old Believers in Russia today are still standing adamant for the very things their seventeenth-century forebears championed, and even died for. Father Avvakum himself was burned at the stake for his part in the Great Schism.

This bitter controversy involved more than semantics, liturgy, and theology. The Old Believers declared Patriarch Nikon was seeking the repudiation of nationalistic forms of worship developed autonomously by the Russian church, that Nikon in his scholasticism and admiration for all things Byzantine was seeking to make the Russian church an exact replica of the Greek church as it existed in Constantinople rather than to permit Russia to fashion its own national patterns of worship and church policy. Therefore the Old Believers' rebellion was an outburst of perfervid nationalism and antiforeignism as well as an acrid disagreement over religious forms and usages. Theirs was an inflexible nationalistic sectarianism.

As a small boy and during early youth Peter often visited the "German suburb" in the capital city, Moscow. The German suburb was an enclave in Moscow where a heterogenous group of recently arrived foreigners lived— German, Swiss, English, French, Dutch. Peter was charmed by the exotic foreigners he met there; he visited them almost daily. The men in the German suburb took a decided liking to the bright young heir-apparent to Russia's throne. They told him of their native lands, of the new industries, inventions, and scientific discoveries in Western Europe. They told him of the great seas and oceans, of navies and merchant marines, of the finding of new and hitherto unheard-of lands and continents.

Young as he was, Peter soon realized his Russia had shut itself off from a fast-moving, yeasty world beyond the borders which hemmed him and his countrymen in. He sensed that new ideas, great ideas, were in gestation in Europe. He resolved someday to visit the lands from which his friends in the German suburb had come, to see for himself the burgeoning world beyond.

And so he did twice, the first journey to Europe in 1697-98. In the meantime, of course, he had been crowned czar, a czar who said his ambition was to "open a window on Europe," who wanted to move his stagnant nation into the modern world. While he was "out west" in Europe, the church at home became very restive over his enthusiasm for things European. The palace guard, the Strelitzi, plotted to put him off the throne because he was becoming too un-Russian. Cutting his tour short, he hurried back to Moscow, tried the Strelitzi for plotting against the throne, executed many of them, and ordered all the rest to shave off their beards. He had found many Europeans clean shaven, so cut off his own beard and ordered all officials around him in Moscow to do the same. This created as huge a furore as if the governor of California would order that the "beatniks" of San Francisco's North Beach should shave and get haircuts!

The church became upset when Peter began ordering foreign books imported into Russia, when he started sending hundreds of Russia's most intelligent young men to study in European universities, when he invited learned Europeans to come to Russia to help him modernize his medieval nation. He was denounced as a "Westernizer," an opprobrious epithet. The Old Believers, fearful their *status quo* views would be shaken loose by the innovators from the West, united with the Slavophiles in calling Peter antichrist. They resented his increasing contacts with the outside world; they wanted Russia to remain forever separate and hermitized.

Peter went into action by abolishing the patriarchate. He appointed a nonchurchman as procurator-general of Orthodoxy. He termed this official "the czar's eye," and an all-seeing eye he was! Through the procurator-general Peter policed the church with a vengeance. It was a union of church and state, with the church on the bottom of the pile. It was the fabled lion and lamb lying down together, with the lamb inside the lion.

Perhaps it is superfluous to say that the church was happy when Peter suddenly died of pneumonia at age fifty-eight, only four years after his abolition of the patriarchate. The pneumonia was induced by an act of heroism: he jumped from his ship into an icy December sea to rescue a man overboard.

We recount the story of Peter and the church to show that Orthodoxy, existing as it did for nearly one thousand years before the Soviets came to power, although always in union with the state, did not always have things its own way. It was often rent by dissension within. It was always fearful of the West and Western ideas; it stoutly resisted every effort to modernize Russia. It became wealthy in estates under serfdom, and therefore resentful of any suggestion of change in the economic status quo, where it occupied a privileged position. It was, indeed, in the best Marxian tradition, a mighty pillar supporting the capitalistic class in Russia. And because of that role it suffered bitterly after Lenin and Trotsky took control the night of November 6-7, 1917.

Religion Survives Under Stalin

Chapter 3

Czar Nicholas II, the last of the Romanovs, was pressured into abdication on March 15, 1917, whereupon a provisional government was established by Prince George Lvov and Alexander Kerensky. The new government, keenly aware that the Russian Orthodox Church was a mainstay of czarism, downgraded the church. Indeed, the March Revolution just about demolished the traditional ideological and political structure of all religious bodies in Russia.

Despite the fact that it had been prorogued before the czar's abdication, the Fourth Duma (national legislature) had established the Council for the Affairs of the Orthodox Church. With this act on the part of the provisional government it was evident that big changes were in store for Orthodoxy. Many of the clergy saw the handwriting on the wall and declared themselves against the erstwhile policies of the church and demanded conformity with many of the goals of the new government. Lvov and Kerensky called such clerics "the Progressive Clergy," declaring that the government would support this group in its drive for changes in the hierarchy. The clerical traditionalists, as might be expected, bitterly castigated the Progressive Clergy, labeling them traitors.

In August, 1917, a Sobor (church council) was convened. This council represented the Old Guard in Orthodoxy, those who were aghast at the new forces surging in Russia which forecast a gigantic revolution in the church as well as in the state.

The 1917 Sobor passed resolutions demanding that the church be altogether independent from the state, that the state must recognize as valid and indispensable the marriage laws of the church, that the state recognize as legal the canonical structure and hierarchy of the church, that the church be recognized as a juridical person (having legal rights in courts of law), that the feast days of the church be recognized by the state as legal holidays, that all holidays be observed with religious ceremonies conducted by the church, that the clergy be exempt from military duty, that the head of the state be a member of the Orthodox Church, that the church have the right to own property and all its property be tax exempt, that the church be supported by state subsidies.

In other words, the Sobor demanded all the rights and privileges enjoyed by the church during the three centuries of Romanov rule. The provisional government rejected these demands instantly and in toto. The Bolshevik organization, which had been formed March 14, 1917, the day before the czar's abdication, and which was led by Nikolai Lenin after his return from Switzerland in April, also derided the demands of the Sobor. It appeared that the traditionalists in the church had altogether misread the signs of the times after the March Revolution.

Only two days before the Soviet Revolution of November 6-7, 1917, the Sobor elected the metropolitan of Mos-

3

cow, Tikhon, Patriarch of Moscow and All Russia. There
had been no patriarchate since Peter the Great abolished
it in 1721. The accession of Patriarch Tikhon represented
a return to the ultraconservative and reactionary views of
the church. The new patriarch lost no time in attacking and
anathematizing the leaders of the Soviet regime, declaring
them "the godless lords of the darkness of this age." [1]

The confiscation of all properties of the church and
of the monasteries was the act which irked Tikhon the
most. These properties, accumulated over the centuries,
represented huge investments in money and art. The monasteries had vast agricultural lands, whose total worth was
so great it was quite incalculable. At the time of the Soviet
Revolution the church and the monasteries together represented an aggregation of wealth unmatched in all Russia.

In Chapter 1 of this volume we excerpted portions
of the decree of January 23, 1918, declaring, "The Church
is separated from the State," with a dozen stipulations in
implementation of those ominous seven words. At this time
the Soviets were led by Nikolai Lenin, ardent Marxist
and avowed foe of religion. Lenin often quoted Marx's
dictum, "Religion is the opiate of the people." Lenin was
a prolific writer, and often he assailed religion in paragraphs such as this:

"Religion is a kind of spiritual vodka in which the
slaves of capitalism drown their human shape and their
claims to any decent life. Marxism is materialism, relent-
lessly hostile to religion. The fight must be linked up with
the concrete practical work of the class movement, which
aims at eliminating the social roots of religion."

The Eighth Congress of the Russian Communist Party
(March, 1919), dominated by Lenin, adopted a program
which read in part:

"With reference to religion, the All-Russian Communist Party does not content itself with the already decreed separation of church from state—i.e., with measures which are a part of the program of bourgeois democracies, but never fulfilled in those democracies because of the many and various ties binding capital with religious propaganda.

"The All-Russian Communist Party is guided by the conviction that only the realization of conscious and systematic social and economic activity of the masses will lead to the disappearance of religious prejudices. The aim of the Party is finally to destroy the ties between the exploiting classes and the organization of religious propaganda, at the same time helping the toiling masses actually to liberate their minds from religious superstitions, and organizing on a wide scale scientific-educational and anti-religious propaganda." [2]

Thus Lenin and the entire Soviet regime were adamant against religion and all its institutions. They had no other purpose but the extirpation of Russian religion root and branch.

Soviet Russia has had three constitutions: the first, the Constitution of the Russian Soviet Federated Socialist Republic (R.S.F.S.R.), 1918; the second, the Lenin Constitution, or Constitution of the U.S.S.R., 1923; the third, the Stalin Constitution, 1936. The Stalin Constitution is the one in force today throughout the Soviet Union. Article 124 of this document reads:

"In order to insure to citizens freedom of conscience, the Church in the U.S.S.R. is separated from the State, and the school from the Church. Freedom of religious worship and freedom of antireligious propaganda is recognized for all citizens."

This section on religion is found in Chapter X, "Fundamental Rights and Duties of Citizens." This chapter comprises Articles 118 to 133 of the Stalin Constitution. It is sometimes said that Chapter X is the counterpart of the Bill of Rights appended to the U.S. Constitution in 1791. However, the Stalin Constitution has some unique features not paralleled in our Bill of Rights. For example, Russia's "Bill of Rights" guarantees to each citizen the right to a regular paying job, the right of rest and leisure, the right to maintenance in old age and in the event of disability, the right to education, the equality of the sexes, the right to no racial discrimination. For the most part the Soviet government has faithfully carried out these guarantees.

But Chapter X also guarantees the right to freedom of speech and of the press, the right to assembly and street demonstrations, the right of personal privacy, including privacy of correspondence and privacy of the home.

These rights, as understood in the Western World, exist only on paper in the Soviet Union. The right of dissent receives short shrift in the Soviet Union, for the monolithic Communist Party, which is the center of power, brooks no interference with its directives or dissent from its ideology. The Party's way is the only way. The CPSU represents the tightest monopoly of power the twentieth-century world knows.

Article 124 guarantees the right of antireligious propaganda, but grants no right to religious propaganda. This is altogether consistent with the Kremlin's view that religion is totally invalid and that eventually it must be completely eliminated from the Soviet Union.

Religion is placed under a terrific handicap when it cannot defend itself against its attackers, when it cannot evangelize and proselytize. The Lenin Constitution of 1923 allowed both religion and antireligion the right to propagandize, but in 1929 that constitutional provision was amended to give antireligion propaganda privileges and to deny the same to religion. Seven years later when the Stalin Constitution was written, it incorporated the 1929 amendment, which canceled out the right of religious propaganda.

This puts religion in the Soviet Union in a most disadvantaged position, for the CPSU campaigns incessantly and militantly against religion, but religion cannot rebut or answer back. It cannot defend itself. The Party presents a thousand arguments alleging religion a myth, unscientific, and historically nothing more than a willing handmaiden of capitalistic exploiters of the working class. Religionists are not allowed to present a shred of evidence in refutation. Their lips are sealed.

As a consequence of this one-sided, one-party debate, the masses of people in Russia who never see the inside of a church, a synagogue, or a mosque do not have the opportunity of knowing anything about religion except from its vilifiers and detractors. In Russia today out of a population of 235,000,000 people about 20 percent are believers in religion. This means that four out of every five persons in the U.S.S.R. have no chance of hearing what the priest, the preacher, the rabbi, and the mullah have to say for the validity and desirability of religion. So far as the Soviets are concerned, two sides to the issue of religion do not exist— just one side, the atheistic side. This is a "heads I win, tails you lose" situation!

The Soviets, however, have been punctilious in carrying out those provisions of Article 124 which guarantee freedom of conscience and freedom of worship. Any Soviet citizen may accept any religion he chooses, or he may flatly reject anything and everything connected with religion. He

may go to the church of his choice and worship there with
fellow believers. The governmental authorities protect that
right fully.

When it comes to freedom of conscience, the conscience
of 80 percent of the Russian people tells them to shun religion. As Karl Marx himself declared, "Conscience does
not determine life; life determines conscience." When most
Russians find themselves in an environment which belittles
religion, their consciences soon tell them they should have
nothing to do with it. Any person's conscience can be
trained to say what that person wants it to say. Twenty
percent of the people have consciences which tell them to
adhere to belief in religion, and they therefore follow their
consciences. This is up to the person. The government pro-
tects the person's right once he has made the choice—religion or no religion.

When the Soviet government on January 23, 1918, only
ten weeks after the new regime was set up, declared the
separation of church and state, it did a praiseworthy thing.
In no land or nation should church and state ever be joined.
God and Caesar each has his own sphere. To fuse these
spheres is miscegenation of the most dangerous character.
The alliance, or misalliance, between the czars and the
church brought nothing but grief to the masses of Russian
people. Therefore, the decree of separation in January,
1918, marks a great day for modern Russia and its peoples.

It is altogether pertinent to ask here, If church and state
are distinctly separate in Russia today, what, if any, rela-
tion exists between the two?

Under the supervision of the Council of Ministers the
state has set up two liaison organizations to handle church-
state relations. Each of these has done, and is doing, a
splendid job of it. No one, except he be a nit picker, will

levy allegations of injustice or prejudice against these two groups. One of these is the Council for the Orthodox Church; the other, the Council for Various Religious Groups. Each of these has a director, who is the mouthpiece of the government. He is, of course, an atheist, as are all government officials under the Soviets; but since the establishment of these Councils nearly a quarter of a century ago, in most cases the director has leaned over backward to be fair in his administration of the laws and regulations of the state as relating to religion. In late 1966 the two Councils dealing with religion were merged into one, the Council on Religion, with Vladimir Kuroyedov as chairman. No basic policy changes regarding the status of religion vis-à-vis the government were made with this merger.

Soviet law requires all religious groups to be registered with the government. Any group of twenty or more Soviet citizens eighteen years of age or more may form an association to satisfy their religious needs and to worship together according to their conscience. Such an association has the right to rent, buy, or construct places of worship. It may have its own workshops for the manufacture of candles and other objects necessary for worship. The clergy of all such associations are supported wholly by the freewill offerings of the members. No religious association may receive money from groups or organizations outside the U.S.S.R., without *ad hoc* permission; this is very difficult to come by. Revenues received by these associations are tax free, but the clergy are taxed on the same basis as all other citizens.

Religious associations may establish schools for the training of their clergy. The Baptists, the most important Protestant denomination in Russia, are allowed to send young men to England for theological training. Muslims have a number of madrasahs (seminaries) in central Asia. On occasion they are permitted to send students to the University of Al Ahzar in Cairo, the most renowned of all Islamic seminaries.[3]

For all religious groups in Russia worship services may consist of sacred music, the liturgy, and sermons. Sermon content is strictly limited insofar as comment on social and political issues is concerned. The preacher may discourse on the Holy Scriptures (for the Muslims, the Koran) to his heart's content, but he must not wander into the field of governmental or controversial secular affairs.

This prohibition has irked many "liberal" religionists who visit the U.S.S.R., for the liberals in Western Christian circles are wed to the "social gospel," believing that the church must become involved and be a participant in all social, political, and international issues of the day, the more controversial the better. The advocates of the "social gospel" condemn the Soviet limitations on sermonizing.

On the other hand, more conservative religious leaders who believe the fundamental mission of the church is the establishment of the principles of the kingdom of our Lord and Saviour Jesus Christ in the hearts of men, to bring sinners to repentance, to induce the regeneration of sinful men by action of the Holy Spirit in a "new birth," hold that the limitation on preaching in Russia is not so bad after all, and may be in conformity with the words of Christ Himself when He said, "My kingdom is not of this world."

I have attended many church services in the Soviet Union—Orthodox, Roman Catholic, Protestant, Jewish, Islamic. To my mind those who conduct the services have not appeared to be under restraint. In all Christian churches they preached the gospel as it is recorded in the Scriptures.

Their sermons are expository, with an appeal to the hearers to live the Christian life as exemplified in Jesus when He tabernacled among men.

However, it seems grossly unfair for religionists of all persuasions not to be able to conduct active evangelism in Russia, seeking to make converts to religion. No association may print or circulate evangelistic literature or publicize its services, inviting and urging people to attend. In recent years the Orthodox Church has been allowed to print a few thousand copies of the Bible. In central Asia, where Islam is predominant, the muftis (religious leaders) have been permitted to print a small edition of the Koran. But all this is but a drop in the bucket; the supply nowhere meets the demand. Many Christians have no Bibles; many Jews have no Old Testaments; many Muslims have no Korans.

On the other hand, printed propaganda in behalf of materialism and atheism is legion. For long years the most aggressive atheistic periodical was *Bezbozhnik* (*The Godless*). This was put out by the League of Militant Godless (LMG), which also published a second periodical, *Antireligioznik* (*Antireligion*). Of recent years a less disputatious monthly magazine, *Nauka i Religiya* (*Science and Religion*), has been issued. Its attacks on religion are on a higher level; nevertheless it gives no quarter. *Bezbozhnik* often went into the gutter for ammunition to hurl at religion.

The League of the Godless was first set up at Easter, 1925. Some of the Communist intellectuals felt too many religious practices and observances were still extant in Russia; hence they wanted an organization that would make systematic warfare on religion. Four years later the organization's name was expanded by one adjective to read, "The League of the Militant Godless," and *Bezbozhnik* was launched. The demand on the part of the intellectuals in the CPSU was to step up the antireligious war. In the meantime, the First Five-Year Plan for the hurried industrialization of the nation had been begun (1927-28). Soon thereafter Stalin and his associates discovered that the farmers were not producing enough food and fibers for the fast-growing industrial population in the cities; they therefore decreed the collectivization of agriculture. The farmers rebelled against having their land taken away from them; this revolt triggered a bitter reaction against the recalcitrant peasants by the Party.

The Party strategists suddenly discovered that religion was faithfully adhered to by the peasants, more so than by the proletarians in the cities. The Party figured if someway the hold of religion could be broken, the peasants would be more cooperative with the government and less rebellious over collectivization. This is the basic reason for the League of the Militant Godless, founded in 1929, which was committed to the de-Christianization of rural Russia. By 1932 the LMG had 5,700,000 members and a very elaborate program for the promotion of antireligion among the peasants. Indeed, in 1932 a Five-Year Program of Antireligion was started by the LMG. Thousands of places of worship were closed up; the country was inundated with atheistic literature; hundreds of lecturers were sent into every nook and cranny of the countryside to attack religion and to boost the philosophy of materialism.

The big campaign of 1932-1937 was a flat failure. By 1937 LMG had only two million members, most of them not among the peasants but mainly in Moscow, Leningrad, and Kiev, the three largest cities. In January, 1937, a national census was taken; much to the amazement and chagrin of the CPSU, approximately fifty million people out of a total population of two hundred million declared themselves believers. Thereupon the government ordered that in future census taking no questions concerning religion be asked.

The bitter attack of the LMG on religion actually aided religion. Multitudes rallied to the defense of religion out of disgust for the methods and unscrupulousness of the LMG. It might have been a case of sympathy-for-the-underdog psychology, but wherever and whenever atheist lectures were given, religion underwent a revival in that area. Indeed, *Krokodil* (*Crocodile*), the Soviet journal of satire and humor, ran a cartoon (February 29, 1960) showing a group of believers down on their knees with their faces uplifted to heaven praying, "O Lord, send at least one antireligious lecturer into our district."

It wasn't too long after the failure of the Five-Year Plan of Antireligion that the leaders of the LMG were arrested and tried for their failure in the antireligion campaign.

At present one of the most active exponents of atheism is the huge Komsomol (Communist Youth Organization). This is made up of college and university youth in the age bracket of seventeen to twenty-five who are the most ardent in their espousal of Marxism and Sovietism. These are they who scoff at religionists, who hold religion not only to be in error but a major barrier to the advancement of Marxism in the twentieth-century world. Komsomol has been given the assignment under the Senior Communist Party of being the vanguard against religion in the U.S.S.R. Komsomol is militantly atheistic; it leaves no stone unturned in its aggressive campaign against the Orthodox Church and all the other religious associations.

Russia is a nation of avid readers—newspapers, pamphlets, magazines, paperbacks, and hardback books. *Pravda,* the CPSU daily paper, has a circulation of seven million, perhaps the greatest in all the world. *Izvestia,* the government daily, also enjoys a mass circulation. There are some ten thousand newspapers in the U.S.S.R., with a total circulation of eighty million copies.

Russia has one of the highest literacy rates in the world. The Soviets claim less than 1 percent illiteracy. Everyone reads, reads, reads. The CPSU sees to it that all reading matter advocates the materialist philosophy while constantly depreciating and denigrating everything religious.

Radio Moscow, the national network, heard twenty-four hours daily throughout all eleven time zones of the U.S.S.R., has a constant flow of material lauding Marxist materialism and pointing out what the CPSU considers to be the faults and errors of all viewpoints based on religion. As television reaches out farther and farther into that vast expanse which is the Soviet Union, it too is employed in the propagation of the Party's views on religion. Thus, the nation with the third largest population in the world (next to China and India) is blanketed day and night with anti-religion. Moscow is the Mecca of antireligion, the world capital of atheism.

Of recent years the Soviet government and the church have achieved a *modus vivendi,* but prior to this agreement for peaceful coexistence there were several rough episodes between those who governed Russia and those who sought to perpetuate religion.

One of the most bitter clashes occurred early in the Soviet era. Russia was hit by a terrible famine in the years 1921-22. This ghastly famine came on the heels of the Civil War and Allied Intervention, which were devastating. These came on the heels of World War I, in which Russia

suffered enormous loss of life, property, and valuable territory. The nation was therefore in a grave economic situation before the famine struck. When the famine hit, millions
faced early death by starvation. Thereupon the Soviet government ordered the confiscation of the church treasures
and their sale for cash to raise money to buy import food.
The church refused to surrender the stipulated treasures,
which consisted mostly of costly vestments, crowns, chal-
ices encrusted with jewels, and other valuables. The refusal was based on the fact that the articles demanded had
been consecrated to sacred use only, that to use them for
barter in the marketplace would be blatant and unforgivable sacrilege.

The church officials were also suspicious that the state,
under the guise of famine relief, was seeking to put religion
out of business entirely by confiscating the sacred vessels
requisite to worship.

Very artfully the state turned the argument against the
church by declaring that the hierarchy would put material
things above human life, that the church officials would
rather see one thousand Russians miserably starve to death
than to turn over one priestly vestment whose sale could
provide food. The net result of this confrontation was a
serious loss of face and status for the Russian Church.

Out of this battle over the treasures of the church there
came a new organization, The Living Church. This was
formed by younger and more progressive clerics in the
nation who believed the older, higher clergy were risking
the very existence of the church itself by their continuous
defiance of the state and anathematization of its officials.
While the older and more conservative clergy were calling
for a restoration of czarism and the pre-Revolution *status
quo,* the younger men in the church came out on the side

of the state. In short, the establishment of The Living Church tore Orthodoxy asunder.

As was to be expected, the state was jubilant over the schism; it immediately sought to exacerbate other differences within the church, and not without substantial success. The Living Church received hearty commendation from the state, which openly encouraged the expansion of its views and policies. Eventually, the conservative antistate church leaders were liquidated or came over to the moderate views championed by The Living Church.

Up to the very day in the spring of 1941 when Hitler launched his perfidious attack on Russia, Premier Stalin and his colleagues on the Politburo gave the Orthodox Church and all other religions a rough time of it. Stalin had long cherished the hope that religion would soon be nonexistent in the U.S.S.R. Its tenacious hold on life despite all the attacks against it mystified and angered Russia's tough premier. He could not understand the survival of religion under a quarter century of continual battering and bludgeoning. He kept on calling for an intensification of the war on religion until 4 A.M., June 22, 1941. At that hour Adolf Hitler, his wartime ally, crossed the border into Russia with a massive attack and with the purpose of conquering Russia by October or November.

Stalin was quite unprepared, both psychologically and militarily, for this assault by his erstwhile "friend." He did not suspect a double cross; in fact, it took far too many days for Stalin to get it through his head that he and his nation were in dire peril. In the meantime the German Wehrmacht, supported by Luftwaffe and Tank Corps, came rapidly eastward toward Moscow, Leningrad, and Kiev. The blitzkrieg was blitzing and "krieging" at a stunning rate. It appeared that Russia was doomed.

It was then that Stalin, the "Man of Steel," sensed that at any cost he must have the support of all segments of his people, and that included all religious groups in the Soviet Union—Orthodox, Uniates, Roman Catholics, Jews, Muslims, Protestants, Old Believers, Buddhists, Shamanists—the whole works! Instantly Stalin reversed himself in his policy anent religious associations. This was not a change in his basic belief in atheism and materialism. His reversal was an expedient in the light of dire necessity. Stalin had no choice if he and his regime were to survive the Nazi onslaught.

Orthodoxy and other religions in Russia quickly rallied to the support of the Soviets in their death struggle with Hitler. The Nazi *Führer* made repeated attempts to woo the loyalty of the Russian churchmen by assuring them he would give full religious freedom when he conquered the atheistic, godless Communist regime of Stalin. Very few rose to his lure.

Orthodox leaders and other religionists strongly endorsed the Soviet defense, blessing the Red army and air force. The metropolitan urged his followers to take up arms and fight, not only for Mother Russia but also in defense of a Christianity which Hitler with his pagan theories and his cult of the pagan god Wotan was threatening.

Not in words alone did the church support the war effort. Church leaders and their members dug deeply into their pockets for an air squadron of fighter planes to contest the control of the skies with the Luftwaffe. The church's squadron was christened the "Alexander Nevsky" after one of Russia's great war heroes of the thirteenth century.

Church members also sacrificed to raise funds for a tank column called the "Dmitry Donskoy," in honor of another of Russia's national heroes. The tank column was turned over to the government by Metropolitan Nikolay in a speech in which he called upon all Russians to engender "a sacred hatred against the fascist robbers." In that same speech Nikolay called Stalin "our common father."

As one result of his wholehearted support of the state in "the Great Patriotic War," Metropolitan Nikolay was given a high post on a governmental commission in November, 1942, the first prelate to be so honored since the Soviet Revolution.

Indeed, soon thereafter a Common Front of the Soviets and the Church was set up for the prosecution of the war. On September 4, 1943, three metropolitans—Sergius, Alexis, and Nikolay—were invited to meet with Premier Stalin in the Kremlin, surely a red-letter occasion for the church! This memorable conference marked a new day for the church under Soviet rule.

On September 8 Stalin announced that the church was to be permitted to elect a patriarch, the Metropolitan Sergius, and to reestablish the Holy Synod, or full church government on its own. Furthermore, said Stalin, the church may resume the publication of the *Journal of the Moscow Patriarchate,* and may open a few academies and seminaries for the training of the clergy. By far the most surprising statement made by Stalin was that henceforth the church was to be recognized as a "juridical person," with full legal rights and entitled to own property. These stipulations are now known as the "Concordat of 1943."

No sooner was this agreement announced than the officials of The Living Church quickly made overtures for readmittance to Orthodoxy. This was a great gain for the church, for when The Living Church merged with Orthodoxy, the latter regained control over some of the finest ecclesiastical edifices in all Russia.

A sixty-two-foot statue of St. Vladimir stands on a hill
overlooking the Dnieper River at Kiev. Here Vladimir ordered Russian people
to be baptized into Greek Orthodoxy in A.D. 988.

One of tw
ancient Armeni
churches, no
abandoned,
the shore
Lake Seva
high in t
Caucas
Mountai
Armeni
Repub
The date on t
church rea
A.D. 81

Baker

Church of t
Resurrection
Leningrad, al
called Chur
of the Bloo
In 1965 t
Soviets decid
to restore t
aging churc
Scaffoldi
surrounds tw
of t
church's towe

Baker

The Leningrad Mosque.

The Uleg Beg Madrasah,
a Muslim seminary, built in
1417 in Bukhara.

Wooden church built by local carpenters in 1708 in the village of Akhimovo in the northern region of Vologda. The church has twenty cupolas.

Kalan Minaret, erected
by Muslims in 1127
in Bukhara.

The Jar Kurgan Minaret in
Termez in the Uzbek Re-
public was built in 1108-09.

Top right,
Tamerlane's Tomb,
constructed in 1404,
is part of the Gur
Amir Mausoleum
in Samarkand.

In 1535-36 this
Muslim seminary, the
Mir-i-Arab Madrasah,
was built. It is
located in Bukhara.

Above, The Uspensky Cathedral,
also called the Cathedral
of the Assumption, is believed
to be the first church
built in the Kremlin, 1474-1479.

An icon, dated from the
thirteenth century. Icons
are peculiar to Greek
and Russian Orthodoxy.

Left, The Cathedral of the
Annunciation in the Kremlin
is now a historical monument.
Many czars are buried
in the cathedral.

Lowell Jes[...]

The tomb of the mother of Premier
Joseph Stalin in the yard of St. David's
Church, Tbilisi, Georgia. She was a
very pious Orthodox believer.

...thedral of
...Sophia in
...ev, mother
...urch of
...thodox
...urches. The
...ndation was
...in 1037.

Religious icon
from the collection
in the Museum
of Icons in
Tbilisi, Georgia.

The bell tower of
Ivan the Great
Cathedral in the
Kremlin grounds.

Baker

Baker

The famous Novodevichy
Monastery in Moscow covers
fifty-five acres. Because of
its walls it is often referred
to as "the Little Kremlin."

Baker

Church of the Vestments
in the Kremlin.

The Monastery of the Holy Trinity and
St. Sergei at Zagorsk, forty miles from
Moscow, is the spiritual and administrative
center for the Russian Orthodox Church.

Jackson Butler

Lowell Jessen

right, St. Basil's Church
Moscow's Red Square.
is currently a museum
antireligion, but is
cially the Museum
Religion.

Cathedral of Alma-
is presently a museum.
nails, steel, or iron
used in its
struction.

Baker

Cathedral of the Archangel
in the Kremlin. The five
Kremlin churches are now
only historical museums.

The very next month, October, 1943, the government established the Council for the Affairs of the Russian Orthodox Church. This Council acts as the go-between in all relations between the state and the church.

The Council maintains a plenipotentiary in every republic, in every diocese, throughout Russia. He is instructed to serve the church in conformity with Russian law.

The Council is also charged with the duty of looking after the interests of the higher clergy. The patriarch is treated by the government as a very important personage. The Council declares the patriarch to have rank equal to the head of any other religious body in the world, including the pope in Rome. The patriarch now belongs to the privileged class in Russian society, a far cry from the early days of the Soviets.

When World War II ended, many throughout the world, and even in Russia itself, said, "Now that Stalin has won the war, he will find he no longer needs the church; it won't be long until he downgrades it as of prewar times."

But Stalin found he needed the church as much, or more, once the war was concluded, for the Soviets had annexed the Baltic republics—Estonia, Latvia, and Lithuania—had taken the eastern half of Poland and some territory from Romania, and was occupying huge areas in Eastern Europe—in fact, west to Berlin and beyond. The Kremlin sat on an uneasy seat in many of these lands. Stalin quickly saw the church could be of great aid in dampening down the fears of the peoples in those annexed and occupied areas. Romania, Bulgaria, and Serbia, for example, were lands where the dominant religion was Orthodoxy. Visits of high church officials from Moscow could do much to allay fear and prejudice against Communist Russia.

5

When in July, 1948, the Russian Orthodoxy celebrated the 500th anniversary of the founding of the church, the Soviet government invited church dignitaries from all over the world to come to the affair, and hundreds did. Moscow, the world capital of atheism, for a few days became the center of Christian interest throughout the world.

After Metropolitan Alexis was elected patriarch in 1945, he and his leading metropolitans often accepted invitations from the Soviets for missions far and near. They were prominent in the Stockholm and Helsinki Peace Conferences, both staged by the Communists. The hierarchs have gone as far afield as Japan and South America on special missions for the Kremlin. Representatives of the Moscow Patriarchate were much in evidence at the Ecumenical Congress in Rome staged by Popes John XXIII and Paul VI.

When Stalin died, March, 1953, the church pulled out all the stops in laudation of the fallen leader. Indeed, prior to this, on the occasion of Stalin's seventieth birthday, the entire episcopate signed a letter declaring Stalin "the faithful defender of the Church," and "leader, teacher, and friend of the toilers."

When Stalin died, the patriarch wrote the Council of Ministers, of which Stalin had been the longtime chairman:

"His death is a heavy grief for our Fatherland and for all the people who inhabit it. The whole Russian Orthodox Church, which will never forget his benevolent attitude toward Church needs, feels great sorrow at his death. The bright memory of him will live ineradicably in our hearts. Our Church proclaims eternal memory to him with a special feeling of abiding love."

The church provided some of its highest officials as a guard of honor as Stalin's body lay in state.

Again it must be emphasized in the interests of truth and objectivity that Stalin's changed attitude toward the church in the Great Patriotic War was one of expediency only. He needed the church and needed it badly in his savage encounter with the invading Germans. On the day he died Stalin was as antireligious in his basic attitudes as ever he had been.

Furthermore, it is to be observed there was also a considerable factor of expediency in the wartime cooperation with the state on the part of the church. The patriarch and his fellows figured Stalin would henceforth be more tolerant toward religion if they were more helpful to him in the war. In this estimate they were 100 percent correct. Each scratched the other's back. Each profited from the scratching.

---

[1] For vivid and authoritative accounts of the confrontation between the church and the Soviets in the early days of the Soviet regime see *Russia: Tsarist and Communist,* by Anatole G. Mazour, professor of history, Stanford University, pp. 599 ff.; *The Russian Revolution and Religion,* by Boleslaw Szczesniak, professor of history, University of Notre Dame, pp. 1-36; *A History of Russia,* by G. Vernadsky, professor of history, Yale University, pp. 406-411; *The Course of Russian History,* by M. C. Wren, professor of history, Montana State University, pp. 637-642; *USSR: A Concise History,* by Basil Dmytryshyn, pp. 126-131.

[2] The volume by Szczesniak already cited, *The Russian Revolution and Religion,* contains a collection of 158 documents concerning the suppression of religion by the Soviet regime in the years 1917-1925. These documents are authoritative. The Szczesniak book also has a seventeen-page bibliography, the most complete to be found anywhere, on religion in this period of Soviet history.

[3] One of the most valuable and reliable books published in the field briefly covered by this little volume is *Religion in the Soviet Union,* by Walter Kolarz. Another volume of great interest is *The Churches and the Soviet Union,* by Constantin de Grunwald. Both Kolarz and de Grunwald have traveled extensively in the Soviet Union. Both are at home in the Russian language. The Kolarz book is compendious. The de Grunwald volume may be a bit too optimistic in its views on the status of religion, present and future, in the U.S.S.R.

CURRENT RUSSIAN
RELIGION

Chapter 4

The Orthodox Church and most other religions in Russia are enjoying far more freedom and autonomy than before the Concordat of 1943. The first twenty-five years of the Soviet regime were difficult for all religions, but the fortunes of religion took a favorable turn after Hitler's attack.

Upon the death of Stalin, March 5, 1953, Georgi Malenkov became premier. Religion enjoyed maximum liberty during Malenkov's tenure. Malenkov was succeeded by Nikolai Bulganin in 1955. In the meantime, Nikita Khrushchev, who upon Stalin's death had become the head of the Communist Party, was fast becoming Russia's new strong leader, although he did not actually take over the premiership until 1958.

At the Twentieth Party Congress, February, 1956, Party Chief Khrushchev delivered the now-famous "De-Stalinization Speech." For eight hours he castigated the dead Stalin as few, if any, men in all the history of mankind have ever been vilified.[1] This speech triggered a general downgrading of Stalin throughout the Soviet Union. Thousands of statues of the premier erected in the fifteen republics were tumbled from their bases and consigned to oblivion. The Stalin entry in the Russian encyclopedia was deleted, as was his name and record from all schoolbooks. Stalin was made a "non-person."

In 1957 and 1958 Khrushchev resumed the militant antireligion campaign which had been suspended by the Concordat of 1943. Some believe Khrushchev did this to show spite toward Stalin for his leniency toward religion in his latter years. Anything Stalin had been for, Khrushchev was against; and vice versa. At any rate, Khrushchev removed G. G. Karpov, longtime Director of the Council for the Affairs of the Orthodox Church. Karpov had always been most helpful and cooperative with church authorities. The man appointed in Karpov's stead had long been known for his bitter opposition to Orthodoxy and other religions in the U.S.S.R. Most of Karpov's associates on the Council were also replaced with personnel who were known to be aggressively antireligion.

Another factor in the antireligion stance of Khrushchev was the world-shaking exploits of Russia in space. In October, 1957, Russian scientists sent into space *Sputnik I.* In April, 1961, Cosmonaut Yuri Gagarin became the first human being to ride a space vehicle far into the heavens and return safely.

These tremendous achievements put Russia far ahead of the United States and other nations in space science. Nikita Khrushchev and the Russian people were justifiably jubilant. Nationalistic pride surged to a new high.

These scientific successes reacted against religion. Premier Khrushchev, for example, gleefully reported, "Russian cosmonauts have gone into the heavens far higher and farther than any others; did they see God while they were up there? No, of course not, for there is no God!"

The Marxist-Leninist-Stalinist line had always been, "Modern science proves religion a myth. In the ages of man's ignorance he called upon his gods to do for him what he could not do for himself. But science will soon be doing everything once thought possible only for God. Men will then discard the very idea of God, for they no longer will feel a need of him."

With Russia's deeds in space, with industrialization making genuine progress in the once-agrarian Russia, and with the standard of living rising, the Kremlin instructed its propaganda forces to trumpet the message that not only is religion a grievous error, but belief in and dependence on God are out of date, for Russian scientists have taken the place of God.

The Orthodox Church and other religions might have had a much rougher time in the days of Khrushchev had it not been that the great alliance between Moscow and Peking suddenly began to disintegrate, much to the dismay of the men of the Kremlin. Mao Tse-tung, China's leader and an ardent admirer of Stalin, took umbrage at Khrushchev's De-Stalinization speech. Later Mao scorned Khrushchev's warnings against the imminent launching of "The Great Leap Forward" program. When, as Khrushchev had predicted, "The Great Leap Forward" became "The Great Flop Backward," Mao was more embittered than ever. No one wants to hear the four biting words, "I told you so." Soon after the debacle of China's Commune system Russia began to withdraw money, credit, and technicians from Peking. Then came the Chinese attack on India; after that Moscow and Peking were not speaking anymore, except in denunciation of each other.

This coming-apart-at-the-seams of the partnership between the two great Communist world powers was a traumatic experience for Khrushchev. This happened just as he was planning to move against religion in the U.S.S.R. with greater severity than ever. Suddenly he had more important things to do than to war on religion.

Khrushchev was dismissed from office in October, 1964. Premier Kosygin and Party Leader Brezhnev, who succeeded him, have been too busy with external and internal problems to do anything but maintain the *status quo* in state-church relations. Religion in Russia therefore is today in a position not too much different from that enjoyed most of the time since the Concordat of 1943.

What is the status of various religious groups in the U.S.S.R. in the post-Khrushchev era? Not many years ago there was held at the Zagorsk Monastery a "Conference in Defense of Peace of All Churches and Religious Associations in the U.S.S.R." The list of churches and associations attending, as furnished by the Moscow Patriarchate, consists of the following groups registered with the government:

1. The Orthodox Church of Russia.
2. The Orthodox Church of Armenia.
3. The Armenian Church.
4. The Roman Catholic Church.
5. The All-Union Council of Evangelical Christians/ Baptists.
6. The All-Union Council of Seventh-day Adventists.
7. The Reformed (Calvinist) Church.
8. The Evangelical Lutheran Church.
9. The Methodist Church.
10. The Old Believers.
11. The Community of Spiritual Christians (Molokans).
12. Muslims (four Regional Councils of Central Asia).
13. Central Buddhist Council.
14. The Jewish Communities.

The Russian Orthodox Church with some twenty thousand parishes and many millions of members is by far the largest and most important of all Russian religious groups. Among Protestants the Evangelical Christians/ Baptists and the Lutherans are the two major bodies. More than sixteen million Muslims are mostly concentrated in central Asia. The Roman Catholic Church and Judaism are small in numbers when compared to the groups just mentioned. The Georgian Orthodox Church is *the* church in the Republic of Georgia, as is the Armenian Church in Armenia. These two are virtually "national churches" in their respective republics. Both Georgians and Armenians have always been proud of their ethnic identity.

Under the sponsorship of Patriarch Alexis the Moscow Patriarchate in 1957 issued a large volume, *The Russian Orthodox Church: Organization, Situation, Activity*. This publication declares the church to be self-governing and altogether independent of the state. Unabashedly it declares the church much better off now than it ever was under the czars. While the church does not have nearly as many adherents today, yet in the conduct of its ecclesiastical affairs it has much more freedom and autonomy than when it was integumented with and subservient to the secular power of the Russian state. It now elects its own hierarchy without dictation or even suggestion by the government, which was never the case before 1917. Here, for example, is one statement from the Moscow Patriarchate:

"Pre-revolutionary Russia knew neither freedom of conscience nor freedom of worship since there existed a system of a State Orthodox Church ruled by the supreme power of the head of the state—the Tsar, who had the right to issue, alter and cancel all in the ecclesiastical sphere that in his opinion was not founded on Holy Writ." [2]

The Orthodox Church has ten schools for the training of its clergy; eight of these are secondary theological seminaries, two are academies for higher theological training. The two academies are located in Leningrad and in Zagorsk, forty miles from Moscow. The seminaries are in Moscow, Leningrad, Kiev, Odessa, Minsk, Saratov, Stavropol, and Volhynia.

Candidates for the seminaries must be at least eighteen years of age, must have a secondary-school certificate, must read with ease the Slavonic texts, must be able to recite a large number of prayers, and must have a character recommendation from the village priest.

In order to be admitted to an academy the candidate must have completed four years of seminary studies and have been graduated therefrom with honors. He sits for comprehensive examinations before admission.

The ten theological schools, their faculties, their students, their physical plants, are all supported by freewill offerings of Orthodox believers. Indeed, not one kopeck in state or secular funds ever finds its way, directly or indirectly, into the coffers of the church. The church now stands on its own feet; this was never true in pre-Soviet times. The church also has sixty monasteries throughout the Soviet Union. The most important of these is the Monastery of the Holy Trinity and St. Sergei at Zagorsk. The patriarch has his official residence there. Zagorsk is the center of Orthodoxy for Russia.

Rated second is the Pechersk Monastery, or Monastery of the Caves, at Kiev. Pechersk is the oldest of all Russian monasteries and in the early centuries of the church was No. 1 monastery in all Russia.

The Novodevichy Monastery (once a convent) in Moscow has played a great role in the history of the church.

For long years it was the exclusive school for the education of the daughters of the nobility. Novodevichy is now a museum. Because of its extensive brick walls it is sometimes called "The Little Kremlin."

Another important religious group in the U.S.S.R. is the Armenian Church, or, in full, "The Holy Apostolic Church of Armenia." Its headquarters are at Echmiadzin, a few miles outside Yerevan, the capital city of the Soviet Republic of Armenia. Armenia is located in the Caucasus Mountains between the Black and Caspian Seas, bordering on Turkey. Mount Ararat, of Noachian fame, is a 17,000-foot mountain in Turkey, but it is only forty miles from Yerevan.

The Soviet Republic of Armenia is all there is left of the onetime independent nation of Armenia, which lay between Turkey and Russia. In World War I the Turks put on a wholesale massacre of the Armenian people. When that war ended, there was no Armenia, for its territory had been divided and annexed to Turkey and Russia. Many Armenians fled to other lands.

Moscow established the Soviet Socialist Republic of Armenia in 1922. As this was the nearest thing to a homeland the hapless Armenian people had, their church established its headquarters at Echmiadzin, where an Armenian Church cathedral and monastery had long existed.

The Armenian Church as now centered at Echmiadzin is the religious headquarters not only for the Armenians in Soviet Armenia and those living in the neighboring republics of Georgia and Azerbaijan, but also for many Armenians throughout the world, all the way from Lebanon and Iran to California. Indeed, 75 percent of Armenians who recognize the Catholicos of Echmiadzin as their spiritual leader live outside the U.S.S.R.

For years after the Soviet Republic of Armenia was founded, the church had a most difficult time. Moscow was determined to minimize the Armenian Church as rapidly as possible, for the men of the Kremlin knew full well that Armenian nationalism and the Armenian Church were intertwined, that in order to make the Armenian people forget their onetime national identity and to Russify them, their religion must be de-emphasized and phased out.

The twenty-year period beginning in 1922 saw terrific pressures put upon the Armenian Church by the Soviets. However, after Hitler's attack on Russia, when Stalin found himself with his back against the wall, the Kremlin soon saw it needed the support of the millions of people in the Armenian Republic, and therefore the Stalin policies which had been aimed at the extirpation of religion in the Caucasus took on a placating pattern toward Echmiadzin.

The Catholicos and his people responded to Stalin's overtures and stood stoutly by the Soviets throughout the Great Patriotic War. In fact, the head of the Armenian Church, Kevork Cheorekchian, prevailed upon his people to dig deeply into their pockets to provide the money for a tank column for the Red Army, which was named after one of the great Armenian heroes, David of Sasoon. Premier Stalin showed his appreciation by inviting Cheorekchian to the Kremlin for a conference in April, 1945, some three weeks before Germany capitulated.

Two months after this historic conference the National Ecclesiastical Assembly of the Armenian Church called for the election of a new Catholicos (head of the church). Delegates came from almost all the Armenian colonies in the world to participate in this election—from the United States, Turkey, Iran, Iraq, Palestine, India, Britain, France, Egypt, Romania, Greece, Bulgaria, Lebanon, and Syria.

And mark this, the Soviet government paid the way for most of these delegates to come to Echmiadzin and entertained them while the conclave was on. This included delegates from the United States.

All that was in June, 1945. In September the Kremlin announced that the Armenian Church would be allowed to open a theological seminary at Echmiadzin, could enlarge its House of Bishops to include clergy of the Diaspora, and could publish a religious journal under the title *Echmiadzin*.

This generous treatment on Stalin's part called for reciprocity by Echmiadzin. In fact, the Kremlin called on the new Catholicos for two actions: (1) The church was to support the demand of the Soviets for annexation of certain Turkish territories on the Russo-Turkish border which were once parts of the nation of Armenia; (2) The Catholicos was to put out a call for Armenians living throughout the world to be repatriated to the Soviet Republic of Armenia, their new homeland.

The Kremlin has often called upon Echmiadzin to help in the Soviets' international policies, such as attending peace conferences and visitations to Armenian colonies here and there over the globe. Three hundred thousand Armenians live in the Middle East, so when the Kremlin mounted its great diplomatic offensive to win friends in the Arab world, Echmiadzin was drafted to help. The Catholicos aided much.

In 1960 the Catholicos visited the United States, Canada, Uruguay, and Argentina in the Western Hemisphere. The Kremlin gave its permission for money from Armenians throughout the world to be sent to Echmiadzin for the enlargement of the seminary there, for repair of Armenian church buildings in the U.S.S.R., and for a printing press.

The Cathedral of Echmiadzin has enormous drawing power for Armenian pilgrims throughout the world. They flock there by the thousands. The cathedral has some of the most priceless ancient church manuscripts extant, beautifully displayed. Indeed, a visit to Echmiadzin is a great experience.

The present Catholicos, Vazgen Balgian, is a Romanian by birth. Until his election to Echmiadzin in 1955, he was the head of the Romanian-Bulgarian diocese. Since then he has become a Soviet citizen and supports the Soviet regime most heartily; so much so, in fact, that some of his clergy outside Russia criticize him for his warm camaraderie with the Communist regime. But in the U.S.S.R., cooperation with the government is the price of survival for any religious group. Believers in Russia feel they are justified in their course of action, for, say they, "did not Christ Himself command, 'Render . . . unto Caesar the things which are Caesar's'?"

Another unique church in the Soviet Union is the Georgian Church. It is altogether separate from the Russian Orthodox Church but has fraternal relations with it. The Georgian Church antedates the Orthodox Church by half a millennium, being established in the first half of the fourth century A.D. Georgia became a part of the czar's empire in 1811. Until the Soviets took over in 1917 the Georgian Church flourished. Before the Soviet period there were some 2,500 congregations in Georgia and twenty-seven monasteries. In the early years of Soviet rule most of the churches and all the monasteries were closed down or destroyed. The Georgian Church underwent terrific repression and persecution by Moscow.

In common with all other religions, however, a more favorable climate was had for the Georgian Church begin-

ning in 1943-44. The head of the church is His Beatitude
Ephraim II, Catholicos-Patriarch. His official residence
and headquarters are in Tbilisi (once Tiflis), the beautiful
capital city of the Caucasus republic of Georgia. He pre-
sides over 150 congregations now. The great sorrow of
the Catholicos-Patriarch is that so few youth in Georgia are
believers. The continual emphasis on the materialist philosophy in the schools has turned most of Georgia's youth
against religion, or, at least, has made them quite indiffer-
ent to its appeals.

One of the amazing aspects of religion in present-day
Russia is the survival of the Raskolniki, or Old Believers.
In Chapter 2 we sketched their split-off from the Orthodox
Church in the seventeenth century. Bitterly persecuted un-
der Czars Alexis and Peter the Great and under Regent
Sophia, they fled the cities of St. Petersburg and Moscow,
settling along the Volga and in the Ural Mountains. Some
went as far east in Siberia as the Mongolian frontier.

After the Revolution of 1905 the Old Believers were
granted partial amnesty. When the Soviets came to power,
the leaders looked upon the Raskolniki with considerable
favor because of the fact that after the Great Schism of
1666 the Old Believers had always been adamantly anti-
czar and anti-Orthodox. Beginning in 1917 they were
granted much religious freedom. There are now one million
Old Believers in Russia, grouped into three hundred parishes. Moscow alone has fifty thousand of these incurably
persistent fundamentalists.

The Old Believers are puritanical in their living; their
diets are simple, their clothing is simple, their houses are
simple. They eschew all vices and are everywhere known
for their sobriety, for their industriousness, for their fru-
gality, and for their deep piety. Being scrupulously honest,

they are often given responsible posts in the kolkhozy (collective farms), in factories, and in offices.

The Old Believers get along with the government perhaps best of all religious communities in Russia, for they do not seek to propagandize or make converts. They worship quietly and unobtrusively; they live apart from all others. Quite puzzling to the militant atheists is the fact that atheism and materialism make no impact whatever on the Old Believers. They seem immune to Marx, but they never lift their voices in opposition to communism. Someone has said, "The Old Believers live in internal exile."

If one were to hazard a prediction, it would be that Old Believers will be around a long, long time in the land of the Soviets.

The largest Protestant group in the U.S.S.R. is the Evangelical Christians/Baptists which may number as many as three million. The merger of the Evangelical Christians and the Baptists came about in 1944. Since World War II the Pentecostals have affiliated themselves with the two merged groups.

The Baptist and Christian Evangelical movements took root in Russia shortly after the middle of the nineteenth century. It was in 1861 that Czar Alexander II issued his famous decree abolishing serfdom. This move on the czar's part discredited the Orthodox Church, which loudly protested freeing the serfs. In reaction against this stand by the church the peasants became receptive to religious ideas other than those of the Orthodox Church. About this time, an agent of the British and Foreign Bible Society, a Scotsman, Melville by name, arrived in the Caucasus and began evangelization. Martin Kalveit, a Lithuanian Baptist, baptized Russians near Tiflis in Georgia in 1867. In contrast to the formal liturgical services of the Orthodox Church

the Baptists emphasized Bible study and group discussion.
They soon gained momentum and members.

The Christian Evangelical movement in Russia was the
fruitage of the work of an English nobleman, Lord Radstock, who made two visits to Russia in the 1870's.
Radstock and his message were received by some of the
most distinguished members of Russia's aristocracy, even
some members of the czar's court. Radstock was joined in
spreading the gospel by two Anglicized Germans, George
Mueller, of Bristol, and Dr. F. W. Baedeker. These three
men had great impact on St. Petersburg, then Russia's
capital city. Some of Russia's most renowned literary figures, such as Dostoevski, Tolstoi, and Leskov, commented
in their books on the spiritual awakening brought about.[3]

Both the Baptists and the Evangelical Christian groups
suffered bitter persecution, exile, and some of the members
even death under Czar Nicholas II up to the year 1905,
when the revolution of that year brought about a degree
of religious toleration. The persecution was, of course, in-
stigated by the Orthodox Church, which could brook no
competition in the field of religion. Between 1905 and
1917 both the Christian Evangelicals and the Baptists made
gratifying headway.

Immediately after the Soviet regime was established,
the outlook for religion became dark, for Lenin and his
colleagues were determined upon the extermination of religion. However, in the famine years of 1921-24 the Soviet
officials discovered that the various Protestant groups,
mostly farmers, were the most productive farmers in
Russia. In a *Pravda* article in 1924 a leading Soviet official
advised that the inefficient Soviet state farms and communal farms be given over to the "Protestant sectarians,"
for "they are the most efficient farmers in Russia today."

This same official cited the fact that the Protestant sectarians had been cruelly persecuted by the czars and therefore deserved the sympathy of the Communist regime.

As a result of these viewpoints freely voiced in official circles the various sectarian groups were allowed, yes, urged, to set up communal farms. The government even gave them financial grants.

The first Protestant sectarian group to set up a communal farm named themselves "The Sober Ones." They were adamant in their stand against alcoholic beverages. In addition to their farming activities they sought to salvage drunkards, prostitutes, and other delinquents by converting them to Christ and Christian living.

The Christian Evangelicals had many farm cooperatives, all of them bearing Bible names, such as Bethany and Gethsemane. In the Caucasus the Pentecostals named their farm "The Commune of the Apocalypse." Seventh-day Adventists had many communal farms in the fertile Ukraine; one was named "The Commune of Brotherly Love," another, "The Kingdom of Light."

But the successes of these Christian farm communes soon aroused the bitter and implacable opposition of the League of the Militant Godless. Those red-hot atheists saw that the Christians in their exemplary living and great agricultural productivity were dulling the arguments of the atheists against religion. The LMG and its parent organization, the CPSU, goaded the government into cracking down on the Protestant groups on the trumped-up allegations that they were engaged in counterrevolutionary activities; that they were spying for Poland, Germany, and Japan; that they were openly propagandizing for religion; that they were influencing Russian youth against Marxism; and that they had bourgeois sympathies.

6

A decree issued April 8, 1929, wiped out many of the privileges granted the Evangelical Christians, the Baptists, the Pentecostals, the Seventh-day Adventists, and others. Soon thereafter came the big new program for the total collectivization of agriculture and the establishment of the kolkhozy and sovkhozy farms, completely government controlled and directed.

All this ended the era of the Protestant sectarian farm cooperatives. As a matter of fact, the 1930's were exceedingly difficult years for any and all religions to survive in the U.S.S.R. Membership fell off, and organizational activities were reduced to a minimum.

However, as we have several times observed in the foregoing pages, when the German military forces swept into Russia in 1941 with their devastating blitzkrieg techniques, the men in the Kremlin soon relaxed their stern proscriptions against religion. Suddenly Baptists, Evangelical Christians, and others were no longer "enemies of the proletarian revolution," but valued allies in the fight against Hitler and his pagan Nazism.

All the Protestant groups profited by the Concordat of 1943. By October, 1944, the All-Union Council of Evangelical Christians and Baptists was formed. This heavy title was in time shortened to All-Union Council of Evangelical Christians/Baptists. In the merger the Evangelical Christians had a preponderance of members. At the present time the Union has some 5,500 congregations in the U.S.S.R., with perhaps three million members, some half million of whom are Baptists. This Union is by far the most influential of all Protestant groups in Russia.

Indicative of the somewhat relaxed attitude of the government toward religion in Russia was the nationwide Baptist Congress held in Moscow, October, 1966. More than seven hundred delegates attended, elected by sixty-three regional and republic conferences of local congregations. The congress was held in the Baptist headquarters and church in Moscow.

At this congress it was reported that since the preceding congress of 1963 some three thousand visitors from thirty-nine countries outside the U.S.S.R. had visited the Moscow headquarters, and Russian Baptists had in the same three years visited the United States, England, Japan, Hungary, the Netherlands, and several other countries. For example, official representatives of the Russian Baptists attended the World Christian Peace Conference held in Prague in 1964, the All-European Baptist Conference in Amsterdam in 1964, the World Baptist Conference in Miami in 1965. Several Russian Baptists were elected officials of the European Baptist Federation.

One of the major agenda items at the Baptist Congress in Moscow in 1966 was preparations for celebrating the centenary of the Russian-Ukrainian brotherhood of Evangelical Christian Baptists scheduled for August 20, 1967, the one hundredth anniversary of the baptism of Nikita Voronin, one of the first communicants.

It was announced at the Moscow congress that an edition of the Bible and a collection of hymns were soon to be printed, and that the circulation of the congress bulletin, Bratsky Vestnik, was to be increased considerably. All this was by express permission of the Soviet government.

Among the smaller Protestant denominations, or associations, in the U.S.S.R. are the Seventh-day Adventists. They have some four hundred chapels or "prayer houses" with approximately fifty thousand membership. In a few of the larger cities, such as Moscow, they meet to worship in quarters assigned to the Baptists. The Moscow congre-

gation has about six hundred members; Kiev and Leningrad about four hundred each. Adventists are rather
numerous in the three Baltic republics—Estonia, Latvia, and
Lithuania. These countries were taken over by Russia in
1940, but in the interval between World War I and World
War II these countries were autonomous, and religion enjoyed great freedom. Adventism grew rapidly during that
twenty-year period. There are many Adventists in the
Ukraine and in the Volga River region, also in Siberia as
far east as Khabarovsk.

Adventism came to Russia through German immigrants and their family connections in Canada and the
United States. Catherine the Great, who reigned from
1762 to 1796, herself a German, urgently invited German
settlers to come to Russia. She wanted their farming skills.
Coincident to the German emigration to Russia was a
considerable trek of Germans to North America. Later,
some of these Germans in Canada and the United States
became Adventists and began sending Adventist literature
published in the German language to their friends and
relatives in Russia. In the 1870's Adventist groups sprang
up in the Crimea, along the Dnieper and Volga Rivers, and
in the Caucasus.

Among the early Adventists in Russia were Theofil
Babienco, Philipp Reiswig, and Gerhardt Perk. In the
1880's L. R. Conradi, of Hamburg, Germany, spent several years in Russia establishing churches in many parts of
the czar's domain. Later J. T. Boettcher expanded upon
Conradi's work. By 1890 Russian Adventists were numerous enough to hold a national convention in the Caucasus.
In 1899 they began to publish pamphlets, periodicals, and
books in Russia to be sold by door-to-door colporteurs.

During the Russo-Japanese War of 1904-05 Adventist

young men were conscripted into the Imperial Army for service in Siberia and Manchuria. Wherever they were stationed, they spread the Adventist message. Later when the czar, at the instigation of Orthodoxy, cracked down on all Protestants, some Adventists were exiled to Siberia. Everywhere the exiles went they furthered Adventism.

For a dozen years after the Soviet regime was established, Protestant groups did not fare too badly. The Soviets were busy curbing the Orthodox Church and paid little attention to the "sectarians." But in 1929 when Stalin bore down on all faiths in Russia, Seventh-day Adventists lost the right to publish and to carry on other types of evangelism.

Since the Concordat of 1943 the All-Union Council of Seventh-day Adventists has been under the supervision of the Council for Various Religious Groups, meaning, of course, all religious groups in the U.S.S.R. except the Orthodox Church, which has a council all its own. Adventists have gotten along very well with the Council. To be sure, Russians have a six-day work week which includes Saturday; this makes it mandatory for Adventists to negotiate for special concessions, and this is never easy. However, no sizable rupture has occurred on this issue. Then again, all Russian children must go to the state schools beginning at age seven and are required to attend six days a week, including Saturdays. Except in rare instances of concession Adventists must comply.

But in the main the Soviet government and the Adventists have amicable relations. These three factors conduce toward this end:

1. Russian Adventists abide faithfully by the government's directive that preaching shall not concern itself with secular affairs, such as social, economic, and political

questions of the day; they concentrate entirely on the exposition of the Scriptures in their sermonizing.

2. From the earliest days of Adventism in Russia many Adventists have been farmers, and exceptionally good farmers at that. During the Stalin regime on more than one occasion the premier commended the high productivity of both the Baptist and Adventist farmers. Inasmuch as the food problem continues to be most vexing to the Russian leadership, those who are outstanding farmers are favorably regarded by the Minister of Food Production.

3. A third factor which enables Russian Adventism to get along rather well with Moscow is that the All-Union Council of Seventh-day Adventists has no connections whatever with Adventist organizations or members in any country outside Russia. Hence they are never accused of "cosmopolitanism," as are Jehovah's Witnesses and the Zionist Jews. In 1928 Russian Adventism severed all ties binding it to Adventist groups outside the U.S.S.R. For nearly forty years Russian Adventism has been completely autonomous.[4]

Since 1940 the Lutherans have been a sizable group in the U.S.S.R. This came about in the second year of World War II when Russia seized and annexed the Baltic republics. Lutheranism had moved into the Baltic region many years before from Germany and Scandinavia. Lutherans are mostly found in Estonia, Latvia, and Lithuania.

Estonia has the one concentration of Methodists in Russia. The Methodists have their own conference and superintendent in Estonia.

The two religious groups which have had strongest opposition from the Soviets are the Roman Catholics and the Jews.

Since that faraway day in A.D. 988 when Russia accepted Eastern Orthodoxy, the Roman, or Western, Church has been regarded as *the* great enemy. Through the centuries the Roman pontiff has repeatedly made overtures to Orthodoxy, seeking a reconciliation and union. These efforts have uniformly come to naught.

A major factor in the deep-seated antagonism of Russia toward Rome is Poland. The Poles early accepted Christianity and through several centuries have been among the most ardent of all Catholics. They still are today. The Liths have also been upholders of the Papacy. The history of Eastern Europe records war after war between the Russians on one side and the Poles and Liths on the other. At times Russia's historic enemies drove deep into Russian territory and held it for decades. Whenever they did, they tried to replace Orthodoxy with Catholicism. This even more embittered Russia against Catholic Poland and Lithuania. When in 1795 Catherine effected the Third Partition of Poland, Russia found herself burdened with millions of Roman Catholics who had been forced to become Russian citizens. Roman Catholics do not give up their religion easily, not even in the face of a ukase from St. Petersburg or Moscow.

Roman Catholicism has always been a minority religion in Russia, but always a source of deep irritation on the part of the czar, who felt Catholics were plotting against him and his regime and against the Orthodox Church. Anti-Catholicism is indigenous to Russia. Every Russian gets it with his mother's milk. Latinophobia is a mental disease which has been endemic for a thousand years.

These anti-Catholic attitudes were stepped up a hundredfold when the Soviets took over in 1917, for no sooner had Lenin and his confreres vanquished the Provisional

Government of Alexander Kerensky than from Rome came stern warnings to Europe and all the world that materialistic Marxism as espoused by the Soviets constituted a threat even greater than those of Genghis Khan, Tamerlane, or the Islamic warriors from the deserts of Arabia. The Roman pontiff poured malediction after malediction upon godless communism.

The years which have come and gone since 1917 have seen little or no diminution in the confrontation between Moscow and Rome. In such Iron Curtain lands as Poland and Hungary collision between Communist governments and Catholic cardinals has been frequent.

The Soviets nurture three basic grievances against Roman Catholicism:

1. Its international character irks Moscow. The Kremlin alleges that Roman Catholics in every land are under the influence and direction of Rome, that Russian Catholics even put the pope above and ahead of the Soviets if the two jurisdictions conflict. This they declare to be the unforgivable sin of "cosmopolitanism"—admiration for and connection with movements and ideologies outside and alien to the U.S.S.R.

2. The Soviets aver that Roman Catholicism with a half billion members in the world postulates the spiritual, the supernatural, and the other-worldly aspects of religion. To Marxist Sovietism such views are anathema; between Marxist materialism and Catholic supernaturalism there never can be any more concord than between Christ and Belial.

3. The Kremlin stoutly maintains there has always been a close connection between Catholicism and capitalism, that this persists even down to the middle of the twentieth century. In Leningrad's Kazan Cathedral, now a

Museum of the History of Religion, a large graphic display was installed in 1965 showing the pope of Rome firmly grasping ropes which reach out over the world and into the largest corporations and banks on the globe. The caption declares that the Roman Church owns shares to the amount of twenty-five billion dollars in these corporations and banks, that therefore the Roman Church and capitalism are so involved one with the other that their identities are inseparable.

There are at the present time some 1,250 Roman Catholic parishes throughout the Soviet Union. Because of the agelong antagonism between Russia and Rome, the state of Catholicism in Russia is far from flourishing. Up to now Catholicism has faced a discouraging future in Russia, but some change seems to be brewing.

The critical issue of world peace, particularly as it impinges on the war in Southeast Asia, has recently brought about a face-to-face dialogue between the pontiff of Rome and high officials of the U.S.S.R. In February, 1966, the Soviet Union's Minister of Foreign Affairs, Andrei Gromyko, had a brief interview with Pope Paul VI in the Vatican. In February, 1967, Russia's head of state, Nikolai Podgorny, chairman of the Presidium of the Supreme Soviet, had an epochal seventy minutes with the pope. The occasion was surrounded by all the prestigious protocol the Vatican could muster, indicating the church's estimation of the importance of the first meeting of the pope with the Soviet head of state since the Communist Revolution fifty years before.

Paul VI and Podgorny discussed two items: (1) possibility of peace negotiations in the Vietnamese war, (2) better treatment of Roman Catholics in the vast territories of the Soviet Union.

The pontiff pointed out that at the present time only two bishops are allowed Roman Catholics in the Soviet Union, and emphasized that this is far too few for servicing Catholic groups over the eight and a half million square miles of the U.S.S.R. Podgorny indicated he believed relaxation of the limitations on Roman Catholics in Russia was desirable.

Even more important was the tentative agreement between Paul VI and Podgorny that there should be set up some sort of special and continuous representation between Vatican City and Moscow whereby continual communication between the church and the Soviets could be had. This would not mean, at least as of now, the establishment of embassies in the respective capitals, but at least a personal representative of the pope in Moscow and a special representative of the Soviet Union in Vatican City would maintain continual dialogue between the church and the Soviet Union.

The pope emphasized his great concern for Catholics living in Ukraine, in Lithuania, and in Latvia. The pope said he hoped his special representative, if and when arrangements were finalized, could visit the sizable Catholic groups in those three republics. Podgorny did not express himself adverse to the pope's pointed suggestion.

President Podgorny told the pope a new constitution for Russia is in the making and that it will include provisions to improve the situation of Catholics in the U.S.S.R.

This historic conference in the Vatican may augur a better day for Roman Catholics in Russia.

Judaism also labors under serious handicaps in Russia today. It is estimated that there are about three million Jews in Russia now. As far as their religion is concerned, the lot of the believing Jew is not one to be envied.

To be sure, the Stalin Constitution of 1936 guarantees no discrimination on the basis of race or nationality. In the main the Soviet government has scrupulously practiced nondiscrimination to a commendable degree. In this respect Soviet Russia has set an example to the world which is worthy of emulation. There is probably less racism in Russia than in any other nation on the globe. This is in glaring contrast to czarist Russia, where anti-Semitism was rife and rampant. Medieval Russia had no anti-Semitism, but after areas of Poland, the Ukraine, and Lithuania became integral parts of Russia, the virus of virulent anti-Semitism came with the new territories, for Poland and other countries in Eastern Europe had long persecuted the Jews.

Once imported into the land of the czars, anti-Semitism soon took root. In the century and a half leading up to the Soviet Revolution of 1917 Russian Jews suffered indescribably. The Jew was a pariah—ostracized, despised, hated.

The Soviet Revolution of November, 1917, changed misfortune and tragedy to good fortune and acceptance for Russia's Jewry. The Jews were no longer confined to ghettos; they were allowed full educational privileges; they were accepted into the professions; they held top governmental positions. Throughout world Jewry went the cry, "Soviet Russia is the new homeland for the Jew, the first real homeland since the Romans scattered us over the world in A.D. 70."

But as the years went by after 1917, there began to be heard talk that the Jew was not integrating into Russian life as he should; that he persisted in maintaining national and racial customs and identities; that many Jews in Russia refused Russification, holding tenaciously to their Jewishness. Some Russian authorities said a major factor in the refusal of the Jew to be homogenized with Russian culture was his religion, that so long as he held onto his religion with a tight grip, just so long would he be going counter to Soviet standards and norms.

After 1948, when the nation of Israel was established, a flood of propaganda was let loose in Stalin's Russia alleging that all Russia's Jews were Zionists. This indictment did the Jews in the Soviet Union great harm, for Zionism in the mind of officialdom in Russia meant dabbling in and supporting Jewish international politics, and this meant Russian Jews were also guilty of cosmopolitanism, a heinous thing in Kremlin opinion. Hence the label of Zionist affixed to a Russian Jew after 1948 was a heavy and onerous load to bear.

Indeed, Premier Stalin developed a phobia when it came to the Russian Jews. Shortly before he died, he became convinced that a group of medical doctors were determined to poison him. He had nine doctors indicted; seven of these were Jews. Stalin termed this episode "the Jewish doctors' plot." Stalin alleged the Jewish doctors had already poisoned to death a number of Communist leaders and were at that very time slowly poisoning him. When Stalin died on March 5, 1953, the doctors were in prison and undoubtedly would have been put to death if Stalin had not died first. Shortly after his death the charges were proved groundless, and the doctors were released.

In the interest of truth and objectivity it must be recorded that some Jews in Russia now occupy high government posts, and some are eminent authors, scientists, lawyers, doctors, and teachers.

On the other side of the ledger, however, it must be emphasized that within recent times it seems certain that the Soviet government has no goal other than the complete secularization and denationalization of all three million Jews in Russia, all this in glaring contrast to the way the Soviets treat other religions and other nationalities in the U.S.S.R. It is painfully evident that the Russian Jew has been singled out for harassment and eventually for the total destruction of his religious and national heritage.[5]

A story in *Look* begins with these paragraphs:

"Throughout the ages, two methods have been used to destroy Jews. The Hitlers and Hamans resorted to cold-blooded murder, while tyrants like the Syrian, Antiochus, tried the more subtle course of religious and cultural strangulation. One way kills the body, the other, the soul. But the objective remains constant: annihilation of the Jews. . . .

"In another 15 years, if present conditions continue, Russia's nearly three million Jews will no longer exist—as Jews. The Soviet Government is making it impossible for Jewishness to survive." [5]

These are the conclusions reached by a team of five religious leaders from the United States who visited Russia in 1966 to study firsthand the plight of Russian Jewry.

The group consisted of Dr. Harold A. Bosley, minister of New York City's Christ Church Methodist; Father Thurston N. Davis, editor in chief of the Jesuit magazine *America;* Father Eugene K. Culhane, managing editor of *America;* Francis E. Dorn, a prominent Catholic layman and former Congressman from New York; and Rabbi Arthur Schneier, of the Park East Synagogue of New York City.

These five eminent men report that whereas in 1956 there were 450 synagogues in the Soviet Union, by 1964 this number had dwindled to 97, and at the time of their visit in 1966, to 62.

"No Hebrew Bibles have been printed for nearly 50

years, nor have any prayer books, except for 3,000 published in 1958. Even in death, a Jew cannot be a Jew. Consecrated burial ground is required by Judaism, but no new land is available for Jewish cemeteries. . . .

"Circumcision *(bris)* of Jewish male infants has become a rarity. In Moscow, only about two are performed a week. But the equally important ceremony of bar *mitzvah*, when at 13 a boy becomes responsible for his own conduct as a Jew, is a thing of the past. There has been only one bar *mitzvah* in Moscow—a city of 500,000 Jews—in the past 15 years."

It must be clearly understood that the current practices of the Soviet government vis-à-vis the Jews is not to be classed as anti-Semitism in the usual meaning of that opprobrious term. It is not a racist policy at all in the context of Hitler's vendetta against the Jews. Nor is it a revival of the onetime policy of the czars toward the Jews with their periodic pogroms, such as the mass massacre at Kishinev in 1903. The Soviet policy today is not one of physical attack; the Russian Jew is not subject to concentration camps and crematoria. Hitlerian barbarism, even in small degree, is not a part of the Kremlin's program for Russian Jews today. Nevertheless the attack on Jewish nationalism and upon the basic religious customs of the Jews continues in Russia—and increases year by year.

Another point merits emphasis: The three million Russian Jews are not asking for special treatment; they simply want consideration equal to that accorded other nationalities and religious groups. They do not ask preferment, only equality. They cannot understand why Muslims and Christians are allowed to carry on essential features of their religions while the Jews are denied the same thing. They cannot understand why the Soviet government al-

lows the many and varied nationalities comprising the
Soviet Union to preserve and perpetuate the identity of
their nationality while the nationality traits and distinctive features of Jewish culture are being discouraged, sup-
pressed, and atrophied.

Let us look a bit more closely at the issue of nationality: In czarist Russia the Great Russians were contemptu-
ous of all other national groups; they let no opportunity
pass to belittle and downgrade anyone who was not a Great
Russian. When the Soviets came to power in 1917, they
sought sedulously to reverse all this. Indeed, the first official recognition of Joseph Stalin came when he was made
Commissar of Nationalities in the Lenin government.
Comrade Stalin was directed by Lenin to go throughout all
Russia from the Arctic to the Black, from the Pacific to the
Baltic, assuring the approximately one hundred peoples
making up the new Soviet Union that thereafter there
would be no discrimination against national groups; on
the other hand, nationality, national traits and customs,
would be preserved intact and, in fact, encouraged and
promoted by the Moscow Central Government. This was a
180-degree policy reversal when compared with the czarist
centuries. This policy became basic and major in the Soviet
regime. Commissar Stalin was ruthless in cracking down
on the slightest evidence of racial and/or nationality discrimination. When he wrote the 1936 Soviet Constitution,
which still governs Russia, he embedded this policy into
law. Article 123 of Chapter X reads:

"Equality of rights of citizens of the U.S.S.R., irrespec-
tive of their nationality or race, in all spheres of economic,
government, cultural, political and other social activity, is
an indefeasible law.

"Any direct or indirect restriction of the rights of, or,

conversely, the establishment of any direct or indirect privileges for, citizens on account of their race or nationality, as well as any advocacy of racial or national exclusiveness or hatred and contempt, are punishable by law."

No believer in civil rights and freedom of the individual in any country of the world can ask for a clearer, more explicit, more praiseworthy guarantee of equality and non-discrimination than the two paragraphs we have just quoted from Russia's basic legal code. We can think of a score of nations, some of them major world powers, who would do well to insert in their constitutions the same two paragraphs.

From that early day in Soviet history when Stalin was made Commissar of Nationalities until very recent years Russia has conscientiously and faithfully carried out both the letter and the spirit of Article 123 of Chapter X. No matter how much one believes communism to be a bad system, no matter how much one may condemn Soviet policy as a whole, yet we must acclaim the leaders and people of Russia for a half century's exemplary example of equal treatment of the one hundred nationalities who live within the Soviet Union. The Kremlin's record in this respect is quite unparalleled in all history.

But now that record is being besmirched and blackened by the current treatment of the three million Russian Jews. All other ninety-nine nationalities and all other religions get scrupulous equality, but not the Jews. They are singled out for increasing attrition of their cultural, national, and religious heritages; they alone are downgraded, denigrated, and doomed. Why?

There are several primary reasons: First, from the viewpoint of international politics the Kremlin is adamantly anti-Israel. In common with world Jewry the Jews of Rus-

The Cathedral of Echmiadzin,
quarters of the Armenian Church
throughout the world, is
fourteen miles from the center
of Yerevan, capital of the Soviet
Republic of Armenia.

Residence of the Catholicos
at Echmiadzin, near
Yerevan, Armenia.

Baker

This is the major Orthodox Cathedral
in Moscow still functioning as a
church. The Patriarch preaches here
when he is in the nation's capital.

The Patriarch Alexis of Moscow
and all Russia heads the Russian
Orthodox Church today.

St. Vladimir's Cathedral in Kiev, once closed by
authorities, is now open for worship again.
The cathedral is crowded at every service.

One of two Roman Catholic Churches in Moscow.

Baker

On Fridays the Moscow Mosque is packed with worshiping Muslims. Several hundred outside listen by loud-speaker.

Baker

Russell St

The front door to the only
Protestant church in Kiev,
the capital of the Ukraine.

People leaving this church service in Moscow are typical Russian churchgoers. The majority are elderly women.

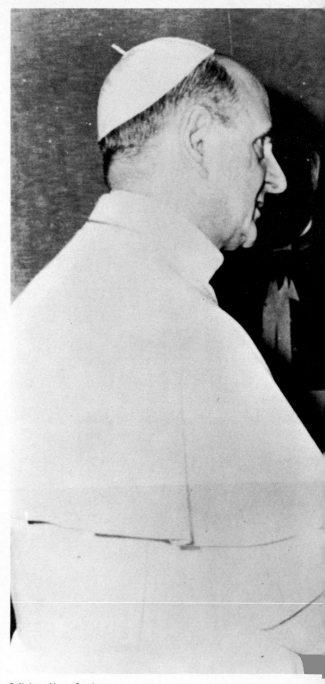

Religious News Service

Pope Paul VI receives President Nikolai V. Podgorny, of the Soviet Union, right, in a historic private audience in 1967, which lasted more than an hour. Podgorny was the first Soviet head of state ever to be received by a reigning pontiff.

The Jewish synagog
in Moscow.

Russell Stevens

A Jewish cemetery in
the ancient city of Samarkand
in the Uzbek Republic.

Alexander M. Demidow,
a Seventh-day Adventist
minister in Moscow.

Two women members
of the Moscow
Seventh-day Adventist
Church are left, Galina,
a medical doctor, and
right, Svetlana, a
graduate engineer.

Moscow Baptists and Seventh-day Adventists
worship in this church. The government
leases it to the Baptists, who sublease to
the Adventists. The church is not far
from Karl Marx Square.

Svetlana Alliluyeva Stalina,
daughter of Premier Joseph
Stalin, as she arrived in New
York City, April 21, 1967.

sia are pro-Israel. This leads the Kremlin to accuse them of cosmopolitanism, which, to the rulers of Russia, is a very serious offense, for to them it indicates a divided loyalty. "The body of the Jew is in Russia, but his heart is in Israel," it is alleged.

But more important in the Soviet view is that the nation of Israel, established in the year 1948, is bitterly hated by the Arab world, and the Kremlin is on the side of the Arab world. When Gamal Abdel Nasser and other Arab leaders declare Israel must be obliterated and the Jews therein drowned in the Mediterranean as Pharaoh's hosts were drowned in the Red Sea 3,400 years ago at the time of the Hebrew Exodus, the Kremlin always voices ardent support of the Arab goal.

To be sure, this attitude is an anachronism, for be it remembered that when Britain gave up its League of Nations mandate over Palestine and turned that land over to the United Nations for disposition, it was the Russian member of the Security Council who made the motion that Palestine be turned over to the Jews of the world for a national homeland! But within hours the Kremlin recognized it had made a colossal blunder, for instant bitter protest broke out in the Arab world against the new nation of Israel; indeed, four Arab nations attacked Israel immediately in a bloody war which lasted for one year but resulted in an Arab defeat and an Israeli victory.

Russia backs the Arab world for the simple reason that the Arab world of the Middle East has the globe's major deposits of petroleum; furthermore, the Middle East from the viewpoint of geopolitics is of the highest political and military value strategically. For centuries Russia has sought to break through Persia and Iraq to the head of the Persian Gulf in order to have access to warm water and the oceans of the world. Later when it became known that the Persian Gulf littoral is the world's greatest petroleum source, Russia's appetite for Persian Gulf control became insatiable.

The rabid bias of the Kremlin against the Jews, and their fervid Arab partisanship, were glaringly evident in the Israeli-Arab war of June, 1967, and in the many pro-Arab speeches given in New York at the United Nations by Nikolai Fedorenko, Andrei Gromyko, and Alexei Kosygin, when the U.N. Security Council and General Assembly debated cease-fire proposals and terms of settlement of the "Sixty-Hour War," which Israel won by a most decisive margin. Even Adolf Hitler never spoke more bitterly against Jewry than did the three Russian spokesmen.

Today the Kremlin feels its international bread is best buttered by aggressive cooperation with the Arabs of the Middle East, and that means relentless antipathy to Israel. Hence it feels any evidence of cosmopolitanism on the part of the Russian Jews, particularly any sympathy for Israel, must be extirpated. One effective way to accomplish this, reasons the Kremlin, is to destroy Jewish nationalism in the U.S.S.R.

How does the Kremlin go about this mission?

One way to destroy Jewish nationalism is to curb and diminish the use of the Yiddish language in Russia. Pure Hebrew has long been forbidden in the U.S.S.R., for the officials declare Yiddish smacks too much of Zionism and international political involvement. Yiddish, of course, is the national tongue of the thirteen or fourteen million Jews in the world. Yiddish is inextricably bound up with all the cultural and historical background of Jewry. Jewish literature, Jewish art, Jewish music, Jewish religion, Jewish education, are all dependent on Yiddish for their virility and perpetuity. The Kremlin knows that the eventual disappearance of Yiddish in Russia would spell the abolition of Jewish nationalism.

Again, the Jews ask no special treatment in regard to their native tongue but merely the same treatment that other national language groups receive in the Soviet Union. All other nationalities are encouraged to use and preserve their languages. Moscow sees to it that in the schools the language indigenous to that group and region is used and taught right alongside the Russian language. Indeed, in *Soviet Life,* the beautifully illustrated magazine published in Moscow and circulated everywhere throughout the United States, the boast is often made that all the nationalities in Russia are encouraged to preserve their languages, declaring that the Soviet government goes to great expense in providing teachers and textbooks in the languages represented by the students.

But not so for the Jew! Despite the fact there are 500,-000 Jews in Moscow alone, not one school in the nation's capital ever hears a teacher use a word of Yiddish. The government wants all Jews to forget Yiddish. On the other hand, such small groups as the Gypsies of Russia, and the Buryats, numbering only a few hundred thousand at most, have their children instructed in their own native tongues with textbooks and reading matter aplenty provided by Moscow.

Then there are the Russian Germans. Centuries ago large numbers of German immigrants came into Russia, and their descendants constitute a major segment of Russia's population. In fact, Germans in Russia represent the thirteenth largest national group. But although Russian Jews constitute the eleventh largest group, they are provided no language facilities in the schools, while the German-speaking group is catered to all over the U.S.S.R.

wherever the German nationals are located. In view of the oft-repeated show of hatred of everything German after the Great Patriotic War, in which Hitler clobbered Russia unmercifully for three years, one would think the Soviet government would play down the preservation of the German language in Russia; on the contrary, Moscow goes to great pains and expense to see to it that every child with German blood in his veins receives daily instruction in his own national tongue.

Most of the major national groups in Russia have their own publishing houses, where newspapers, periodicals, and books are printed in their native tongue. But not the Jews. Before the founding of Israel in 1948, the Jews had many national theaters in Russia, and they had a Yiddish publishing house, which issued a spate of newspapers and other literature. There were many schools in which Yiddish was one of the two languages taught and used (the other being Russian), but no more. After Israel came into being, Stalin sought to wipe out all Jewish cultural institutions. Later Nikita Khrushchev carried out the same anti-Jewish policies.

Thus, when dealing with a Jew, the most effective way to de-Jew him is to emasculate his religion, for the Jewish religion is the taproot of all Jewishness. Therefore, since 1948 down to the present moment the Soviet government has persistently followed a policy of making it more and more difficult for Russia's Jews to practice their religion. By making smaller and smaller the number of cattle to be slaughtered kosher style, by making it more and more difficult to obtain matzoth (Passover bread), by discontinuing the yeshivas (schools for the training of rabbis), by pressuring against circumcision and *bar mitzvah,* by closing up most of Russia's synagogues so that most Russian Jews have no synagogue within reachable distance from their homes—by these and other means the Jewish religion in Russia is being strangled to death. This is national death, not by the bullet or the bake oven, but by attrition.

All this is in glaring contrast to the generous treatment and privileges increasingly allowed Orthodox Christians, Protestant Christians, Catholic Christians, and the Muslims of the U.S.S.R. Their lot is appreciably better than in the period between the Soviet takeover in 1917 and the Great Patriotic War. But not for the Russian Jew; his lot is harder to bear now than in any other period of Soviet history. As he looks forward to the next decade or two, he sees nothing ahead but darkness and the extinction of his nationality and his religion. Physically he may not become extinct, but he will no longer be a Jew. The basic human right of a meaningful identity is increasingly denied him. So far as Jewish culture is concerned, he will become a nonperson, a Russified individual without even a trace of his own distinctive characteristics. Soviet Jewry is undergoing atomization. The Kremlin's persistent policy is to erode the Jewish spirit and to eradicate Jewish values.

The Soviet government contends it is not discriminating against the Jews at all. It alleges that young Jews, and even the middle-aged, are not interested in preserving the old religion or most of the traditions and heritages of former times. It contends that the newer Jewish generations in Russia regard much of Jewry as an anachronism, that they feel the Communist way of life has emancipated them from the myths and superstitions of their grandparents, and that adherence to Jewishness is a major handicap to success and achievement under the Soviet regime. In other words, the government says the younger Jews in Russia are fast becoming secularized and therefore are not even slightly interested in the preservation of the Yiddish language, the Jewish religion, and other distinctive marks of Jewish nationality. Edwin A. Roberts, Jr., a news editor of *The National Observer,* wrote in the February 13, 1967, issue, after a survey tour in the U.S.S.R.:

"The strategy of government propaganda is to cast suspicion on the social usefulness of religion—all religion except Marxism—without defaming all religion directly. The state is generally portrayed as a benign observer, tolerant of religious superstition so long as such superstition doesn't get out of hand. The implication is always that intelligent, modern people are nonbelievers.

"The strategy is effective. Young people with any ambition at all know the practice of religion will retard their careers. They will be typed and considered unstable and not quite loyal. Because most young people seek acceptance as intelligent, modern citizens, they are content to adopt atheism, or at least to keep their true beliefs hidden in their hearts."

The last religious group to be considered is the Muslims. There are at least sixteen million Muslims in Russia; some authorities place the figure at twenty million. Although the great concentration of Muslims is in Soviet central Asia, yet they are widespread. Moscow has 100,000 Muslims, Leningrad 40,000, both cities far from central Asia.

But in the six republics of Azerbaijan, Kazakhstan, Turkmenistan, Uzbekistan, Tadzhikistan, and Kirghistan Islam is professed and practiced by most of the inhabitants. This Islamic area reaches from the western shores of the Caspian all the way to Western China's Sinkiang Province.

The fabled city of Tashkent, the capital of the Uzbek Republic, is the seat of the Muslim Jurisdiction for Central

Asia. This Jurisdiction is divided into four Directorates, each headed by a mufti. The four Directors are located in Tashkent, Ufa, Baku, and Buniask.

There are now 180 mosques in central Asia, with additionally many hundreds of small houses of worship called *makkalin*.

The Muslim people are very generous in the support of their religion. They have recently completed two beautiful new mosques in Tashkent. The Soviet government is spending large sums of money in restoring Islam's historical monuments in Samarkand, Bukhara, Khiva, and Tashkent. These include mosques, tombs, and madrasahs (theological seminaries). Some of these buildings now undergoing restoration are among the most beautiful edifices in all the world. These holy places of Islam include the Gur Amir Mausoleum, the Registan Ensemble, the Shah-i-Zindah complex of mausoleums, and the Bibi Khanum Mosque, all in Samarkand; and the Uleg Beg and Mir-i-Arab madrasahs in Bukhara. [6]

Wars and earthquakes have played repeated havoc with these Islamic monuments. The work of restoration now being done by the Soviet government is most praiseworthy.

Of recent years the Directors by permission of the Soviet government have printed some 10,000 copies of the Koran. The government also charters planes each year to fly pilgrims to Mecca.

Two madrasahs are in operation now, one in Tashkent and the other in Bukhara. They accept male students twenty to forty years of age, who study for nine years to become mullahs (priests). The Koran is the principal source of education for mullahs. A few who show great promise are sent to the Islamic University of Al Azhar in Cairo.

Islamic believers in the U.S.S.R. have not always had it

as good as now. From the days of the Soviet take-over in 1917 down to the midyears of World War II, they were under severe repression. The policy of the Kremlin toward Islam in that time was not a consistent one, but the policy was uniformly anti-Muslim.

Russian communism declares Islam to be the creation of Arab merchant capitalism, representative of the age of feudalism. A Soviet Islamic authority, Professor Lutsyan Klimovich, has described Islam thus:

"Islam is an anti-scientific reactionary world concept, alien and inimical to the scientific Marxist-Leninist world concept. Islam is in opposition to the optimistic and life-affirming materialistic teaching; it is incompatible with the fundamental interests of the Soviet peoples; it prevents believers from being active and conscientious constructors of the Communist society."

When the Soviets took over in 1917, they knew that sometime they would have to deal with Islam in the Caucasus and Turkistan, but realizing how deep-seated are Islamic law and Islamic teaching, and how very zealous all Muslims are in their religious convictions, Lenin counseled a policy of tolerance toward Islam until the new government had dealt with the Orthodox Church and other religious groups in Russia. In other words, Lenin was not sure just how to proceed to root out Islamic belief, so he postponed the day of reckoning.

In the early years of the Soviets, Islamic leaders split as to their attitudes toward communism. The Muslims in central Asia, where conservatism has always been the order of the day, were vehemently anti-Communist. The muftis and mullahs there wanted to fight the Communists—not a war of words, but actual physical combat. But in some other sections of the Soviet Union the Muslims were more moderate, counseling a policy of cooperation with the Soviet leaders, not merely stark opposition on everything. These were called the New Mosque Muslims in contrast to those in central Asia, who were dubbed Old Mosque Muslims.

When the League of the Militant Godless staged the great atheistic offensive of 1928-29, the government moved to abolish Islamic law and Islamic education everywhere throughout the Soviet domain. A large number of mosques were closed, all madrasahs were closed, and the number of mullahs drastically reduced. Mosques were changed over into public schools, clubs, cinemas, and reading rooms. Some mosques were converted into hotels, some into prisons, some into museums. For years the Muslims suffered greater repression than did any of the Christian groups.

When Hitler invaded Russia, however, the fortunes of Islam, along with other religions, took a sharp turn for the better. Stalin knew he could not afford to have all central Asia in revolt against him, with Hitler rampaging deep into Russian territory. Stalin appealed to the muftis to back his war of defense. Most responded immediately. Indeed, their declarations of support were so effusive they gained the nickname of "the Red Muftis." These canny Muslim leaders sensed the great opportunity to put Stalin in their debt and thereby gain acceptance for Islam in the postwar era. Their strategy worked.

After the war Stalin found the Red Muftis most valuable in the expansion of amicable relations between the Soviet Union and such Islamic lands as Egypt, Syria, Iraq, and Saudi Arabia. These muftis soon spread the word throughout the Mid-East and North Africa that Muslims in the U.S.S.R. were enjoying real religious freedom.

When the Cold War began, these same Red Muftis issued pronouncements against "Imperialist America and England." When the Korean War broke out in 1950, the muftis protested "American warmongers" and "American barbarians" in Asia. The muftis employed the radio to blanket the Mid-East and Africa with broadcasts in Arabic praising the Communist Party line in international affairs.

Premier Stalin responded by reopening hundreds of mosques. Since his death in 1953 Russia's leaders have continued a policy of tolerance toward Islam. The city of Tashkent, the center of Soviet Islam, now has seventy mosques in operation, seventeen of them large edifices. On important holy days as many as ten thousand men worship at the Tillah Sheikh Mosque, where the Chief Mufti of central Asia officiates.

But don't think that everything is rosy for Russia's Muslims. Komsomol and other atheistic organizations, including the prestigious All-Union Society for the Dissemination of Scientific and Political Knowledge, wage constant propaganda against the religion of Islam. Their attacks are aimed mostly at such Muslim practices as veils for their womenfolk; the rite of circumcision, often performed unhygienically; pilgrimages to the sacred tombs; the Muslim aversion to swine raising; the Muslim feast days and holy days.

These customs are all peripheral to the real core of Islam—the Koranic teaching of one God, a loving and compassionate God, a God who someday will sit in judgment on men and nations, punishing the unbelievers and rewarding the believers. These are the basic beliefs Soviet atheism is out to destroy.

Will the Soviets someday move drastically for the elimination of all Islamic belief? Probably not as long as the Arab world is vital to the Kremlin's foreign-policy goals.

[1] For the text of Khrushchev's fiery speech see Basil Dmytryshyn's *USSR: A Concise History*, pp. 401-444.

[2] *The Russian Orthodox Church: Organization, Situation, Activity*, Moscow Patriarchate, 1957, p. 22.

[3] The book by Walter Kolarz *Religion in the Soviet Union*, already cited, contains detailed and authoritative accounts of all religions extant in Russia today. The Kolarz volume is the best in the field.

[4] For a detailed account of Seventh-day Adventism in Russia see the *Seventh-day Adventist Encyclopedia*, pp. 1344-1362.

[5] See "Time Runs Out for Russia's Jews," *Look*, November 29, 1966; "The Jews of Silence," *Saturday Evening Post*, November 19, 1966; "A Report and Analysis of the Status of Soviet Jewry," a special issue of *Congress Bi-Weekly, A Journal of Opinion and Jewish Affairs*, December 5, 1966.

[6] A priceless volume, with 135 color plates, titled *Historical Monuments of Islam in the USSR*, was published recently in Tashkent by the Editorial Department, Muslim Religious Board of Central Asia and Kazakhstan. The text accompanying the gorgeous illustrations is in Arabic, Russian, French, and English. This volume is invaluable to students of Islamic history and art.

the future of

religion in russia

Chapter 5

The Union of Soviet Socialist Republics is geographically the largest nation in all the world, reaching from the Pacific on the east to the Baltic and the Black on the west, from the long Arctic littoral on the north to the Hindu Kush and Caucasus Mountains in the south. But gigantic as Russia's eight-and-a-half-million-square-mile domain is, even larger yet is the interrogation mark looming over the "land of atheism," the question mark asking, What sort of future does religious belief and practice have among the Soviets?

We have already declared that the oft-affirmed goal of the men in the Kremlin is the total eradication of religion. For years Russia's militant atheists have been mystified and angered over the fact that so many millions of their countrymen still are ardent believers. A spokesman for one of the aggressive antireligion groups in 1964 said, "Religion in any and all forms must be completely done away with by 1984." Russia's leaders often announce time goals for what they hope to do; more often than not the target year comes and goes with only a percentage of the goal reached. The leaders of atheism may see 1984 come and go with even less realized than those who so often declared that by such-and-such a date the U.S.S.R. would surpass the U.S.A. in industrial and agricultural production.

But the truth is that religion has been living on borrowed time in Russia since midnight, November 6-7, 1917. At that moment the cannon on the cruiser *Aurora,* anchored in Petrograd's Neva River, boomed the start of the Communist take-over. That shot heard around the world also signaled the doom of religion in the U.S.S.R. as far as the avowed intention of the Bolsheviks was concerned.

It is true that the Constitution of 1936 guarantees freedom of worship and conscience, and it is true that the Concordat of 1943 gave religion a new temporary lease on life, but this is not religious freedom in the Western sense. The Soviet policy is one of watchful waiting and of toleration only until death removes the older generation of Russians and universal education for the youth will remove the last vestige of "religious superstition." Complete eradication of belief in God is the one unvarying goal of Soviet Russia, whether it be the Orthodox God, the Roman Catholic God, the Protestant God, the Islamic God, or the Jewish God— all must go into oblivion.

In the meantime, however, the Soviet government has been faithful in carrying out the Constitutional guarantee of freedom of conscience and worship. At the same time the Soviets have laid down guidelines for religious associations, such as no religious propaganda, no evangelism or proselytism, no public meetings or demonstrations, no religious education of the youth except privately in the home, no preaching on social, economic, or political issues, no congregational worship services except in registered churches, mosques, synagogues, and "prayer houses."

Some religionists feel these guidelines are far too restrictive; and, of course, they are, according to the accepted standards in our Western World. But it is idle to argue about that, for Soviet Russia is a nation founded on the ideology of Marxist materialism, with atheism a major plank in its philosophy. If you and I were Soviet Communists, we would confine religion to duly appointed places of worship, too! From the viewpoint of the Kremlin it is most liberal in allowing freedom of religious worship, if on a temporary basis only.

In the meantime religion is not doing too badly in the Soviet Union, for mark this: There are 47,000,000 believers in Russia, or 20 percent of a population of 235,-000,000 people. In Russia you must have courage and conviction of the highest order to declare yourself a believer, for the fashionable thing, the voguish thing, the "in" thing, is *not* to be a believer. There are no "nominal," no "fair weather," believers in Russia. One has to have intestinal fortitude to declare himself a believer in the Land of the Hammer and the Sickle.

In short, belief in God is far from dead in Russia. Some Protestant clergy in the Western World may unctuously declare God dead, but 47,000,000 believers in the Soviet Union know God is alive, for He lives in their minds, their hearts, their souls. This believing multitude is made up of Christians, Jews, Muslims, and Buddhists; their hold on God is solid and enduring, even more enduring than the crenelated walls of the Kremlin.

"But," you ask, "what about the news coming out of Russia now and then which tells us of the arrest and prosecution of religionists in Russia?"

Yes, there are such, but note that nine times out of ten the believers have exceeded limits plainly stipulated by

Soviet authorities. For example, in the summer of 1966 there came to light the instance of six Baptist preachers sentenced to prison for conducting a public baptism of forty persons in the River Don near Rostov. The ministers were charged with staging a religious rite in public, of operating an underground clandestine printing press on which publications were turned out by the thousands, ostensibly to persuade Russian youth to reject communism and become Christians.

If the charges be true, then those sentenced to prison had no valid defense, for Soviet law clearly prohibits public religious convocations and rites, and allows no publication of religious material without express permission.

To keep the record straight, the news stories said the offending ministers were not of the regular Evangelical Christians/Baptists, but a group who had split off and which allowed its zeal to exceed its prudence. The Evangelical Christians/Baptists rarely, if ever, run afoul of Soviet law. Whether they agree with it or not, they abide by it.

While it is true that Christianity, like Islam, is an aggressive, missionary-minded, evangelism-oriented system, yet when a Christian group finds itself in Soviet Russia today, it gets much further by obeying the law than by flouting it. It is quite unfair to allow antireligious propaganda while disallowing religious propaganda, but that is Soviet law; those religionists in the U.S.S.R. who obey the law get much further in their own religious life than those who defy the law. After all, the most effective sermons ever given are the daily lives of godly religionists.

In Russia the Jehovah's Witnesses and the Pentecostals are often hailed before the courts for their extreme pacifism. Articles 132 and 133 of the Stalin Constitution of 1936 read:

"Universal military service is law. Military service in the armed forces of the U.S.S.R. is an honorable duty of the citizen of the U.S.S.R. To defend the country is the sacred duty of every citizen of the U.S.S.R."

One can defend his country without bearing arms by doing noncombatant duty in uniform. We have many such in the armed forces of the United States. But some members of the two above-mentioned groups refuse to have any part in the defense of the U.S.S.R. The Russians are most sensitive on the issue of pacifism, for they had much trouble with the Doukhobors, a split-off sect from the Old Believers. Not only did the Doukhobors refuse any type of military service, but they also refused to pay taxes on the basis that some of the tax money was used for military purposes. Finally, the main body of the Doukhobors left Russia for western Canada, where they were most troublesome to the Canadian government in both world wars. More recently most of them have gone to South America.[1]

Religionists who obey Soviet law have little or no trouble with the authorities.

What of the future? Will the present policy of quasi-freedom toward religion be continued, or will it be abandoned for another era of rigorous and aggressive war on religious belief?

The Scriptures declare, "Thou knowest not what a day may bring forth." Man's fallibility on predicting the future is too well known to need emphasis here. Hence any attempt to foresee developments in religion in the Soviet Union must rely on a parallel with recent trends in the evolution of Marxism there.

The changes in Soviet Marxism since 1917 are spectacular and significant. Most of them have taken place at the expense of orthodox Marxism. When Peking accuses

Moscow of "revisionism," it has plenty of grounds for that allegation, for Russia's leaders have transformed and are transforming the Marxism of early Soviet days.

In 1935, for example, Premier Stalin adopted the policy of Stakhanovism, which allows differentials in awards and wages based on the quality and quantity of production by the individual worker. This was in direct defiance of the Marxist-Socialist dogma, "From every man according to his ability, to every man according to his need." Stalin struck out the word "need," and substituted "productivity," which is, of course, a basic concept of capitalism.

In Khrushchev's time, and now continued under Kosygin and Brezhnev, the policy of Liebermannism prevails— ascertaining by polls what John Q. Public wants in the way of consumer goods, and then producing those goods for him; in other words, asking the public, not telling the public—another capitalist way of running business.

Very pertinent to the discussion is the complete turnabout by the Soviets on marriage, divorce, and the family. In the early days of the Revolutionary regime divorce and remarriage were made very easy, very quick, very inexpensive. One could take a spouse or get rid of one simply by going to the registrar's office, putting down three rubles (seventy-five cents), and signing a legal paper. Anyone having three rubles and a pen could marry and divorce as many times as he wished. If minor children were involved, the state would take the children and rear them in state institutions.

The intent of this system of quickie marriages and quickie divorces, which would turn Reno green with envy, was to destroy the family institution as it had long existed in Russia. And all this was in conformity with the Marxist teaching that the family was controlled by the church for the benefit of a capitalistic society. Marx said that in order to deal the church a lethal blow and to do away with the right of inheritance (parents passing property on to their children), the sanctity of the family and the durability of the family institution must be broken down.

"Down with bourgeois morality," early became one of the slogans of the Soviet Revolution. Sexual freedom almost to the point of abandon was openly advocated and practiced. Under the Soviets, Friedrich Engels' volume *The Origin of the Family* became a best seller overnight. Engels, you will remember, was Marx's collaborator on *Das Kapital*, finishing that work after Marx died in 1883. In *Origin of the Family* Engels attacked the institution of monogamy, declaring it hopelessly bound up with private property rights and capitalism. Engels said monogamy is in denial of the personal rights of the individual, who should be allowed to make love to anyone, anytime, without legal restriction or public disapproval.

Aleksandra Kollontay (1872-1952), a close friend of Nikolai Lenin, and his associate in the establishment of Sovietism, was the author of two volumes, *Love and Friendship* and *Communism and the Family*. She took positions even more avant-garde than Engels'. She lampooned the monogamous family and decried the authority of parents over children as "bourgeois."

In the 1920's and early 1930's moral standards in the Soviet Union went down, down, down. The nation took on a Mardi Gras pattern. Everyone lived it up as his fancy liked. Sex was wherever you found it and whenever you wanted it.

Suddenly in June, 1936, the entire picture changed. New laws were promulgated, making divorce expensive and time-consuming. Abortion, which had been legal and free of fees, was declared illegal. Motherhood and the family institution were lauded to the skies. Common-law marriages, then legion, were discredited and condemned. Puritanical standards for the Soviet people which outdid the New England Puritans of the seventeenth century were affirmed. The government declared youth must remain continent until marriage; after marriage no sex outside the conjugal relationship.

July, 1944, saw another spate of enactments making divorce most difficult to come by. Divorce in Russia today is a matter of court action only. The courts are very loath to grant divorce—both parties must be present in the court. For the seven million residents of Moscow an application for divorce must be published in one of two designated Moscow papers, and the minimum waiting time for the publication of divorce notices is four months owing to the small space allowed in the newspapers for divorce proceedings. The 1944 law also made divorce very expensive —up to $200 for the first divorce, much more for any succeeding divorce.

The court which first hears a divorce complaint cannot issue a decree of separation; that must be done by other, higher courts. Court action may go on for many months. For parents with minor children the divorce process is practically endless.

Soviet judges talk much on the topic of *krepkaya semya*, the "strong family"; they are actually loath to break up a family unit which they believe should be maintained "until death do us part." They emphasize that the family is the cornerstone upon which Soviet society is structured.

All this constitutes the most astounding reversal of policy which Soviet history records.[2]

Far be it from us to try to draw an exact parallel

between the Soviet views on the family and its stand on religion, but we do feel it is reasonable to believe that inasmuch as the Kremlin has discarded some of its key principles on the family institution, it is possible in the decades ahead that it may also tone down its antireligion view. And it is not only on the family that the Soviets have switched, but also on salient features of Marxian economics and Marxian internationalist theory. In other words, Soviet Marxism has undergone, and is undergoing, major metamorphosis.

Lest you say that the supposition that the Soviets may change their adamant stance on religion someday is nothing more than wishful thinking, let us give one concrete example which indicates the Kremlin is most sensitive to world public opinion in the field of religion.

In a visit to the Soviet Union in 1958 I was taken by Intourist to Leningrad's Kazan Museum of Anti-Religion. An English-speaking guide spent two hours conducting us through the onetime cathedral, now wholly devoted to exhibits reviling and derogating religion—particularly the Christian religion, Orthodoxy, and the Roman Catholic Church being the major targets. Kazan is the cathedral where Catherine the Great was crowned, where Alexander I spent the night in prayer before he went out to do battle with Napoleon Bonaparte a century and a half ago. On the average, Kazan has four thousand visitors daily.

In Kazan one sees a large mural depicting hundreds of peasants carrying a golden cross on top of which sits a fat capitalist smoking a huge cigar, who horsewhips the peasants as they trudge along a path following the figure of Christ. On the lower floor of Kazan are shown all the horrors of the Spanish Inquisition, with life-sized human figures being tortured to death by the clergy. All the instruments of torture are shown in gruesome array—the Iron Maiden, the racks where men and women were slowly pulled apart, "martyrs" being burned at the stake.

Galileo's church trial for his belief that the globe is spherical, not flat, is shown as graphically as anything in Madame Tussaud's Wax Museum in London.

But believe it or not, by 1965 Kazan had its name changed to the Museum of History and Religion, and it is no longer on the Intourist schedule of things for foreign visitors to see in Leningrad. When in the Kazan museum in 1965, I asked for an English-speaking guide; I was told none was available, only Russian-speaking guides. I found as I walked through the museum that captions and descriptive matter which in 1958 were in Russian, French, and English were now in Russian only.

Why the change?

Knowledgeable foreigners long resident in Russia told me that the Soviets finally realized that foreign visitors to Kazan went home to tell their countrymen about the bitter attitude of the Soviets toward religion, and how disgusted and revolted they were with the gross caricatures of Christ and Christianity at Kazan. This set up a bad reaction in the Christian world against the Soviets, and inasmuch as the Soviets are most anxious these days for tourists to visit Russia, the Kremlin decided to soft-pedal Kazan. To be sure, Kazan gets a big play from the Russian people themselves, for the government urges its own citizens to visit Kazan, particularly Russian schoolchildren and youth.

This change of policy on the part of the Kremlin is symptomatic of Soviet sensitivity to criticism for its anti-religion views. As the Kremlin tries more and more for "peaceful coexistence" with the non-Communist world, it is logical to believe that it may further soften its attitude toward religionists in the U.S.S.R. Lest this observation be misunderstood, let us again emphasize that such a change of policy is not representative of any basic alteration in the Soviets' view on the validity of atheism, but for expediency's sake the Kremlin may continue to play down its onetime program of antireligious propaganda and repression and give religion more toleration and latitude than even now.

But suppose it does not; suppose, on the other hand, that bitter confrontation on the Cold War and diplomatic fronts between the capitalistic and socialistic worlds eventuates in actual physical war, that in ultimate defiance of the Western World the Kremlin decrees the utter destruction of religion and religionists in Russia, then what future for religion?

No matter how remote the probability of a situation such as just described, any objective forecast must consider its possibility, for it must be borne in mind that Soviet policy is most variable. While longtime Communist goals are inflexible even to the point of dogma, yet the tactics of reaching these goals are like the tides on the seashore— continually in ebb and flow.

In view of the possibility someday of an all-out drive to crush religion beyond salvage, two queries arise:

Is communism capable of exterminating belief in God?

Is man's innate yearning for God extinguishable?

This writer believes the answer to both these interrogations is a resounding NO: in Russian, NYET!

Why? Because over and over again in six thousand years of recorded history attempts have been made to destroy faith and belief; up to now not one such attempt has ever succeeded. Why then believe the Kremlin and the CPSU can do it now?

The most noteworthy example of total failure in this endeavor occurred nineteen centuries ago when the Roman officials, the Pharisees and the Sadducees, and the screaming mob who shouted "Crucify Him! Crucify Him!" left Calvary's hill late that black Friday afternoon. Those implacable foes of the Nazarene were absolutely certain that with the death of Jesus His new, disturbing religion would soon be forgotten. "Jesus is dead, and so are His ideas," they remarked one to another smugly as they headed toward home and supper.

The history book reports that Christianity was born, not aborted, the day Jesus died. In the place of a few dozen fearful followers cringing at the foot of the cross, Christian believers number one billion today, ten times more than the population of the entire globe on the day of the crucifixion. And mark this—despite a half century's campaign to eradicate Christian belief, millions of Christians still live and worship in the U.S.S.R.

Another example of the eternal longevity of belief in God is the Jew. Scattered to the four winds by mighty Rome in A.D. 70, nineteen hundred years later fifteen million Jews throughout the world still celebrate Rosh Hashanah, the Day of Atonement, and Passover as their forefathers did before Diaspora. Even the genocidal attempt of *Der Führer* to extirpate the Jew with all the barbarism of Dachau and Auschwitz failed to close ten thousand temples and synagogues throughout the world where the Jew still worships and adores his monotheistic God.

Walter Kolarz recounts the true story of the Rabbi of Lyubavichi, who suddenly found himself face to face with three members of the Soviet secret police, who burst into the synagogue to arrest the rabbi for alleged infraction of directives on religious practice. When the police confronted the rabbi with drawn guns, the rabbi coolly declared he would not cease his religious duties no matter what. One of the police, pointing his gun directly at the rabbi, reminded him that his gun had changed many a man's mind. The Rabbi of Lyubavichi replied, "Your gun may intimidate that sort of man who has many gods and many passions, but only one world. I have one God, and I have two worlds; therefore I am totally unimpressed by your gun."

When Svetlana Alliluyeva Stalina, daughter of the late Premier Joseph Stalin, landed at Kennedy Airport, New York City, on April 21, 1967, she read a statement which declared in English, "I have grown to believe it is impossible to exist without God in one's heart."

This categorical statement dropped like a nuclear bomb of a million megatons upon our world! Here was the 42-year-old daughter of one of the most resolute and dedicated atheists the world has ever known witnessing to that basic religious truth—the indispensability of belief in God. What a stinging rebuke to Russia's Communist Party, to the Young Communist League, to the League of Militant Godless, and to the hundreds of thousands of teachers in the vast educational system of the U.S.S.R., who every day tell their students, "There is no God and no validity to religious belief. Only the ignorant and stupid believe such things."

Svetlana Alliluyeva Stalina is representative of the intelligentsia in Soviet life today, many of whom are in revolt against the lack of freedom of thought and expression under the Communist regime. She is a university graduate and would undoubtedly have made Phi Beta Kappa and Phi Kappa Phi had she gone to one of our colleges. Yet she makes the flat statement, "It is impossible to exist without God in one's heart."

The testimony of Stalin's daughter has demolished the case of the Communists against religious belief. Be sure that in the far reaches of the Soviet Union there are millions living under the Hammer and the Sickle who have found the same God as has Svetlana Stalina.

Belief in God is unkillable. Even Joseph Vissarionovich Dzhugashvili Stalin, who ordered five million Russians to their death when they resisted collectivization of agriculture, and who sent double that number to exile in Siberia, even that same Stalin could not banish God from the heart of his own daughter, Svetlana!

In explanation of why in 1962 she became a member of the Russian Orthodox Church Svetlana Alliluyeva said, "One cannot live by bread only." This statement, a quote from Jesus Christ Himself, is a flat rejection of the philosophic doctrine of materialism, the cornerstone of Marxism. Thus within minutes of her arrival in the United States Svetlana dealt a death blow to both materialism and secularism. And that death blow, mind you, was delivered by the daughter of Joseph Stalin!

[1] For an authoritative account of the Doukhobors see *Terror in the Name of God*, by Simma Holt.
[2] For a detailed account of "Morals, Marriage and the Family" in the U.S.S.R., see the chapter with that title in the very valuable volume by Maurice Hindus, *House Without a Roof*. Hindus has written a half dozen volumes on Soviet Russia, all excellent.

Bibliography and Suggested Readings

Anderson, Thornton, *Masters of Russian Marxism*. New York: Appleton-Century-Crofts, Inc., 1963.

Bach, Marcus, *God and the Soviets*. New York: Thomas Y. Crowell Co., 1958.

Bissonette, Georges, *Moscow Was My Parish*. New York: McGraw-Hill Book Co., Inc.

Braun, Leopold L. S., *Religion in Russia From Lenin to Khrushchev*. Paterson, New Jersey: St. Anthony Guild Press.

Central Committee of the Communist Party of the Soviet Union. *History of the Communist Party of the Soviet Union.*

Charques, Richard D., *A Short History of Russia*. New York: E. P. Dutton and Co., 1956.

Curtiss, John Shelton, *The Russian Church and the Soviet State, 1917-1950*. Boston: Little, Brown and Co., 1953.

de Grunwald, Constantin, *The Churches and the Soviet Union*. New York: The Macmillan Co., 1962.

Deutscher, Isaac, *Stalin: A Political Biography*. New York: Oxford University Press, 1949.

Dmytryshyn, Basil, *Medieval Russia: A Source Book, 900-1700*. New York: Holt, Rinehart and Winston, 1966.

——————, *USSR: A Concise History*. New York: Charles Scribner's Sons, 1965.

Ellison, Herbert J., *History of Russia*. New York: Holt, Rinehart and Winston, 1964.

Fainsod, Merle, *How Russia Is Ruled*. Cambridge, Massachusetts: Harvard University Press, 1963.

Fedotov, Georgii Petrovich, *The Russian Church Since the Revolution*. London: S.P.C.K.

Fisher, Marguerite, *Communist Doctrine in the Free World*. Syracuse, New York: Syracuse University Press.

Fletcher, William C., *A Study in Survival: The Russian Orthodox Church, 1927-43*. New York: The Macmillan Co., 1965.

Florinsky, Michael T., *Russia: A History and an Interpretation*. New York: The Macmillan Co., 1953. (2 vols.)

——————, *Russia: A Short History*. New York: The Macmillan Co., 1964.

——————, *Toward an Understanding of the USSR*. New York: The Macmillan Co.

Gsovski, Vladimir, *Church and State Behind the Iron Curtain*. New York: Mid-European Studies Center.

139

Harcave, Sidney, *Readings in Russian History.* New York: Thomas Y. Crowell Co., 1962. Vol. I, From Ancient Times to the Abolition of Serfdom. Vol. II, The Modern Period.

————, *Russia: A History.* Philadelphia: J. B. Lippincott Co., 1959.

Harper, Samuel N., *The Russia I Believe In.* Chicago: University of Chicago Press.

————, and Thompson, Ronald, *The Government of the Soviet Union.* Princeton, New Jersey: D. Van Nostrand Co.

Hazard, John N., *The Soviet System of Government.* Chicago: University of Chicago Press, 1960.

Hearnshaw, F. J. C., *A Survey of Socialism.* New York: The Macmillan Co.

Hendel, Samuel, *The Soviet Crucible.* Princeton, New Jersey: D. Van Nostrand Co., 1963.

Hindus, Maurice, *House Without a Roof.* Garden City, New York: Doubleday and Co., Inc.

Holt, Simma, *Terror in the Name of God.* New York: Crown Publishers, Inc.

Hunt, Carew, *The Theory and Practice of Communism.* New York: The Macmillan Co.

Jones, Dorsey D., *Russia: A Concise History.* Harrisburg, Pennsylvania: The Stackpole Co., 1955.

Kirchner, Walther, *A History of Russia.* New York: Barnes and Noble, Inc., 1955.

Kolarz, Walter, *Religion in the Soviet Union.* New York: St. Martin's Press, Inc.

Lenin, V. I., *Lenin on Religion.* New York: International Publishers.

Marx, Karl, *Capital: A Critique of Political Economy.* New York: The Modern Library.

Mazour, Anatole G., *Russia: Tsarist and Communist.* Princeton, New Jersey: D. Van Nostrand Co., 1962.

Moorehead, Alan, *The Russian Revolution.* New York: Harper and Row, Publishers, Inc., 1958.

Moscow Patriarchate, *The Russian Orthodox Church: Organization, Situation, Activity.* Moscow: Moscow Patriarchate.

Muslim Religious Board of Central Asia and Kazakhstan, *Historical Monuments of Islam in the USSR.* Tashkent, Uzbekistan.

Pares, Bernard, *A History of Russia.* New York: Alfred A. Knopf, Inc., 1953.

Pipes, Richard E., *The Formation of the Soviet Union.* Cambridge, Massachusetts: Harvard University Press, 1954.

Pollock, J. C., *The Faith of the Russian Evangelicals.* New York: McGraw-Hill Book Co., 1964.

Ruhle, Otto, *Karl Marx: His Life and Work.* New York: The Viking Press.

Salvadori, Massimo, *The Rise of Modern Communism.* New York: Holt, Rinehart, and Winston, 1963.

Schapiro, Leonard, *The Government and Politics of the Soviet Union.* New York: Random House, 1965.

Schuman, Frederick L., *Soviet Politics at Home and Abroad.* New York: Alfred A. Knopf, Inc.

Schwartz, Salomon M., *The Jews in the Soviet Union.* Syracuse, New York: Syracuse University Press.

Scott, Derek J., *Russian Political Institutions.* New York: Frederick A. Praeger, Publisher.

Seventh-day Adventist Encyclopedia. Washington, D.C.: Review and Herald Publishing Association, 1966.

Shuster, George N., *Religion Behind the Iron Curtain.* New York: The Macmillan Co., 1954.

Skousen, W. Cleon, *The Naked Communist.* Salt Lake City: Ensign Publishing Co., 1961.

Spector, Ivar, *An Introduction to Russian History and Culture.* Princeton, New Jersey: D. Van Nostrand Co., 1961.

Spinka, Matthew, *Christianity Confronts Communism.* London: Religious Book Club.

——————, *The Church and the Russian Revolution.* New York: The Macmillan Co.

Szczesniak, Boleslaw, *The Russian Revolution and Religion.* Notre Dame, Indiana: University of Notre Dame Press, 1959.

Timasheff, Nicholas S., *Religion in Soviet Russia, 1917-1942.* New York: Sheed and Ward.

Towster, Julian, *Political Power in the USSR.* New York: Oxford University Press.

Treadgold, Donald, *Twentieth Century Russia.* Chicago: Rand McNally and Co., 1959.

Tucker, Robert C., *The Soviet Political Mind.* New York: Frederick A. Praeger, Publisher, 1963.

Turner, John K., *Challenge to Karl Marx.* Reynal and Hitchcock.

Utechin, Serge V., *Russian Political Thought.* New York: Frederick A. Praeger, Publisher, 1963.

Vernadsky, George, *A History of Russia.* New Haven, Connecticut: Yale University Press, 1961.

Walsh, Warren Bartlett, *Readings in Russian History: The Revolutionary Era and the Soviet Period.* Syracuse, New York: Syracuse University Press, 1963.

——————, *Russia and the Soviet Union.* Ann Arbor, Michigan: University of Michigan Press, 1958.

Webb, Sidney and Beatrice, *Soviet Communism: A New Civilization?* London: Longmans, Green, and Co. (2 vols.)

Williams, Albert Rhys, *The Russians.* New York: Harcourt, Brace, and World, Inc.

Wren, Melvin C., *The Course of Russian History.* New York: The Macmillan Co., 1963.

Periodicals

Congress Bi-Weekly, special 48-page edition, December 5, 1966.
Look, November 29, 1966, pp. 100 ff.
Saturday Evening Post, November 19, 1966, pp. 38 ff.
Soviet Life, February, 1967, pp. 64, 65.